D0546833

Books by Solara:

11:11
Inside the Doorway

EL*AN*RA:
The Healing of Orion

The Star-Borne:
A Remembrance for the Awakened Ones

The Legend of Altazar:
A Fragment of the True History of Planet Earth

Invoking Your Celestial Guardians

how to
LIVE
LARGE
on a small planet

· SOLARA ·

To all my Lost Loves...

eternally melted together
in the vast Ocean of Love,

cast adrift
in the Sea of Silence.

Star-Borne Unlimited
111 Glen Lake Dr.
Eureka, Montana   59917
(406) 889-5288

First Edition published June 1996
Second Edition published October 1996

ISBN #1-878246-32-1

Living Large:

To physically embody

the vastness of the Invisible

on a daily basis
until it becomes
our New Normal.

This book is written from my personal experience. . .
An ongoing journey into the deeper Invisible which is still
in motion.

All I know anymore is that nothing is certain. Nothing is
preordained or carved in stone. Even our most sacred
Truths can be instantly replaced by infinitely vaster Truths.
And our very cells are constantly being recalibrated as we
birth new levels of our True Selves.

Civilizations rise and fall.
Stars are born and die away.
Beloved Loved Ones come and go.
The passing of the seasons.
And throughout it all, we endure. . .

We fall and then we rise.
We dare to Love again. And again.
After awhile, the rising and the falling
become the same unified motion.
We Love no matter what—
simply because that's who we are.

From my own experiences, I have finally learned to accept
not knowing—to find comfort in the great emptiness of
the Invisible—to set aside my fine old tools which no longer
serve—to embrace the raw vulnerability of my Core Self—
to be wild & free wherever I am—to Love deeply with everything I've got—and to welcome each day as if it were
both the first and the last.

• TABLE OF

• THE KEYS TO THE INVISIBLE •

CONTENTS.

Living in an Unreal World

We are living in strange times in an unreal world. Life has become so out of balance that we now consider the extreme aberrations of these times as normal. All the elements of our lives have been greatly distorted.

*We have forgotten how to live
and we have forgotten how to love. . .*

Now our unreal world is beginning to crumble. The vast underlying corruption and decay is finally being brought up to the surface where it can be clearly seen. Everywhere we look something is dying away; someone is calling out in anguish. Our hearts have been repeatedly broken. Our cherished dreams have been crushed. Our value systems are revealing their hollowness. Our religions have become dusty and controlling; many of our churches have become either social clubs or mausoleums for a dead past. Our ancient Gods have become impotent and the all-mighty God of money, selfishness and greed reigns.

We have continuously butchered and raped our environment until it has been irreparably damaged. We have lost our connection with the natural world. And most importantly, we have lost our respect for ourselves by living lives of compromise and denial.

Our relationships are often shallow, dysfunctional and unsupportive, still mired in the mud of karma, jealousy, neediness and guilt. Incomplete personality selves trying to find wholeness with other incomplete fragments. Instead of true courtship, we have heartless seduction based on selfishness and lust rather than love. We've replaced the sacredness of making love with phone sex, cybersex and sadomasochism. Rather than risking deep intimacy, we enact dull role playing with our partners and our children. We cocoon ourselves with false family values that only stifle true kinship and closeness, limiting the free expression of our love to a narrow group of people. As parents, we avoid living out our dreams until our children grow up, then discover that we've forgotten how to fly.

We are just hollow shells of our True Selves endlessly going from one illusory dream to the next. Such is our unreal life in an unreal world.

Look around you, anywhere, and you will see rampant corruption and distortion. In many areas of the world women are still treated as chattel and ethnic minorities are oppressed. Impersonal, technical medicine that treats the symptoms, but does not heal. Education which fails to teach us how to learn. Politics which no longer serves the needs of the people. Businesses whose bottom line is profit rather than quality, which not only don't serve the consumers, but exploit their workers. Even our holidays have become commercialized clichés, tired exercises of meaningless ritual. We seek to fill the emptiness of our lives with entertainment whose most popular genres glorify violence and sexual exploitation.

We've even lost touch with the naturalness of our physical bodies, allowing them to either be neglected, abused or over developed.

Many of our leaders in every field, our current role models, are motivated by overblown egos and a lust for power. We avidly follow the minutest details of their lives rather than concentrate on our own. Our supermarkets are full of food which isn't even real. Some of it started out as real before we added pesticides, additives, preservatives, and irradiation. Then we take this "food" home and nuke it in our microwave ovens, washing it down with our chemical soft drinks. We have polluted and poisoned much of our water supply until there is very little pure water left. This natural water is sold in fancy bottles as a special commodity. At night we sit passively in front of our little boxes called television, tuning out rather than tuning in. To cope with all of this, we imbibe alcohol and drugs which further anesthetize our painful loneliness.

Through it all we keep busy, busy—going from distraction to distraction like well trained robots, keeping ourselves numb to the underlying, all pervading emptiness which constantly surrounds us. Feeling lost and unworthy, disempowered and alone. Adrift in the confusing chaos of a warped world. Chattering superficially with friends, focusing on our careers, fighting with our families, making money to pay the rent. What else could we possibly do?

Of course, some of us are on spiritual paths. We have a Divine Mission to fulfill. We have acquired more elaborate kinds of distractions, trading up to a higher illusion. Giving ourselves over to the guidance of spiritual hierarchies or gurus, wearing our crystals, chanting our mantras, speaking with soft voices, communicating with UFOs, channeling anyone other than ourselves. It's still an illusion and we're still living in an unreal world. . .

There's a New World waiting to be born.

This book is about reality. About waking up and becoming Vibrantly Alive. About stepping free of our illusions. About finally learning not only to Love, but to BE LOVE. Living our lives in a constant state of wonder and sublime ecstasy. And grounding our vastness into our enlivened physical bodies by Living Large on this small planet.

Our greatest challenge is to become real.

If we can become fully alive, stripped to the core, true, vulnerable, natural, deep, wide open, passionately loving, whole beings, then perhaps, we can step beyond the confines of this dying, unreal world and create something New.

There is a new world waiting to be born. There is a Greater Reality right in front of us. The membranes to this Greater Reality are dissolving at this very moment. The veils are lifting. The doorway is open before you. . .

A most

practical manual

to become

Vibrantly Alive!

The Greater Ascension

There is much talk about ascension these days. Numerous books have being written on the subject. Every few months it seems that there is yet another planetary activation or opening of another stargate. Theories abound ranging from UFO intervention to the liberation from our physical bodies. Where is this impending ascension going to take us? Possibly to a huge spaceship or another dimension or to a new Greater Central Sun System. Everyone seems to have a part of the key, yet all this profusion of information doesn't quite flow together into a unified whole. Thus there is massive confusion concerning the truth of ascension.

**Many of us feel that
this is our last lifetime on Earth.**

We are bringing our long cycle of incarnations to a close. We know that this final lifetime is an important one. Now is the time to complete all unresolved karma. We need to step into wholeness by integrating our shadow selves, healing our emotions and clearing out all those elements within our beings which keep us from openly being our True Selves. In addition, each of us has a Divine Mission to fulfill. We are all here for a reason. We know that we are going through a tremendous amount of restructuring for some Higher Purpose. This transformation and recalibration is taking place on the core cellular levels of our being, severely affecting our physical, mental, emotional and spiritual bodies. Our Light Bodies are being activated and we know that we will need them to survive.

There is also the growing realization that we are in the Time of Completion, the final days of duality. Many of us can feel the life-force slipping away from duality. Once solid matter is becoming increasingly transparent. The reality of duality is dissolving. Suddenly the life we have been living, our old selves, our old value systems have become transparent and lifeless. They no longer feel real. At the same time, the gap between who we really are and who we embody in daily life is becoming increasingly uncomfortable. We desperately want to bridge this gap and experience wholeness.

A dull emptiness settles in. . .

Do you remember when we were younger in far more innocent times, when the world was full of myriad places to visit or live, when our career choices were many, when this world was filled with infinite unlimited potential? This new sense of duality's hollowness isn't merely a symptom of advanced age or maturity. It is felt by all those who are awakened beings, regardless of age or experience. There are many young people just starting out on their life's path who feel this emptiness as well. They look about at their diminished options, trying to create a future which feels exciting and real, yet find nothing which offers the possibility of true fulfillment. Everything feels flat, dull and known, as if we had already done it all before.

A profound sense of weariness covers us like an encroaching mist pulling everything into its thick embrace. Often it's as if the colors are draining out of life, revealing the unrelenting starkness of black, white and gray. Senseless wars abound in this era of random violence, widespread corruption and underlying fear. Where is the vibrancy, the bounteous joy of living? Where is a future in which we can live as ecstatic beings filled with Love and optimism?

One thing is certain:
We will no longer find our future
or our fulfillment within the old Template of Duality.

We won't find the security we seek within our crumbling value systems. We won't find the depth of Love or the nourishing relationships for which we yearn. We won't even find our True Selves—for duality is the land of illusion. Here in the Time of Completion, duality is dying away daily. During these final days, we will see much that has previously been hidden in the darkest crevasses of our souls and within our collective planetary unconscious brought up to the surface to be cleansed, healed and transformed. At last, the mist of illusion is being dispelled and illuminated.

This is definitely a most challenging time to be alive. Yet, we would do well to constantly remember that each of us chose to be alive right now, not only to experience the final days of duality, but to serve as midwives and instruments of Divine Intervention to shift the evolutionary template of planet Earth. We are here to facilitate the quantum leap from duality to Oneness.

How do we make this shift, living in such an unreal world? First, we must make it within ourselves. We must loosen and let go of all which keeps us hooked into duality. We must shake free of the false limitations of time and space, unpinning our beings so we can live in the eternal state of No-Time. We must transcend karma by stepping into our vastness. Most importantly, we need to embody a deeper, truer level of Love found in the One Heart.

There is a New World waiting to be born.

It must be experienced in our physical bodies on this physical planet. And it waits for us to birth it. This new world is known as the Greater Reality. It is located in a frequency band of energy which we call the Invisible. The Invisible is all around us right now. If we want to discover our new futures, if we want to be vibrantly alive and loving, if we want to live in the New as New Beings, then we must learn how to explore the Invisible.

The Spiral of Duality

The Spiral of Duality is the evolutionary path we have taken since first arriving upon this planet.

This spiral of evolution is defined by the parameters of the Template of Duality which means that we are subject to the laws and limitations of time, space, polarity, separation and karma. Polarization is the key. Everything is defined by its opposite pole: male-female, night-day, good-evil, love-hate, black-white, rich-poor, happy-sad, oppressor-victim, win-lose.

We have been so embedded with the polarity of duality that most of us believe it to be true. We feel that if something good happens to us, that we will have to pay back our happiness later when something bad will inevitably happen. Polarities are the cornerstone of the Template of Duality. This is unquestionably true, yet what many of us don't yet realize is that there are levels of consciousness *far beyond duality* which are available to us right now. And in these vaster realms, polarity doesn't exist except as faded memories within a much greater whole.

Another distinguishing feature of the Spiral of Duality is that everything is perceived from the physical realms of matter. *"If it appears on the physical, it is real."* The opposite of this would also be seen as true: *"If it's not on the physical, it's not real."*

Physical manifestation is the predominant definition of reality for the Spiral of Duality. Here, one's vantage point would be standing on the surface of the Earth gazing outwards horizontally. We are not aligned with Earth or Star. Almost all our attention is placed on other physical phenomena. Success and happiness on this spiral are often defined and measured by what we can amass on the physical realms such as: money, career, family, an attractive or successful partner, house, car, possessions, and our own physical appearance. We put a lot of our attention on achieving and holding onto these desires.

The Spirituality of Duality

Our horizontal focus is sometimes altered when we have "spiritual" experiences. For example: when we pray—we look upwards, going outside of ourselves to a higher source; when we meditate—we look inwards; when we contemplate—we receive an overview. Most of the old, established religions on the Spiral of Duality are for the purpose of giving us peace of mind or partial enlightenment within the established parameters of duality. Many of them simply give us something to follow, so we don't need to think for ourselves. *The primary motivation of organized religions is not to liberate us from duality, but rather to maintain duality as the predominant paradigm of reality.* The same could also be said for much of what is labeled "New Age" spirituality. Its goal is not to awaken us into true Oneness, but rather to awaken us from one dream so we can embrace another illusion.

Planetary Activation

The Great Awakening: into what?

In August 1987, there was a massive planetary activation called the Harmonic Convergence. Hundreds of thousands of people participated worldwide and anchored the Fourth Dimension. This event served to awaken many to previously unexplored spiritual dimensions and levels of awareness. Around this time there was a huge explosion of New Age philosophies. A profusion of people began channeling everything from their own Higher Selves to disincarnate entities, dolphins, Angels, space beings, ancient warriors and Ascended Masters.

Suddenly, there were myriad new teachings, processes and information to assimilate. Many of us had not yet honed our skills of discernment and in our great excitement at reawakening, welcomed everything with enthusiastic openness, forgetting to run it through our own individual truth filters. Yes, we belonged to the Ashtar Command, Great White Brotherhood and Mikael's Legions! We were also Angels, incarnate unicorns, space commanders, Gods & Goddesses, shamans and who knows what else!

It was starting to get confusing. . .

For such a long time we had been aligned with the horizontal energies of secondhand knowledge and now here we were, opening up to new vertical energies and being overloaded! What many of us didn't realize is that since the Fourth Dimension had merged with the Third, much of this new input was emanating from the astral planes of illusion. Some people *were* aware of this, but didn't mind, since these new energies were infinitely more interesting than what we had known before.

In the midst of this psychic barrage and spiritual revival, information was received concerning our impending ascension.What people often forget is that channeled information is only as accurate as the level of consciousness of its source. Even if it originates from *the Highest* or from God him/herself, is this *Highest* emanating from the Spiral of Duality or that of Oneness?

Much will also depend on the clarity and awareness of the human person who is doing the channeling. Although the channel might be contacting a pure Source, how that energy is interpreted, stepped down and communicated into the physical will totally depend upon the level of awareness of the one receiving the transmission. This is an area of much distortion and misinterpretation of information. Remember that game called Telephone we used to play as children when we would whisper a message around a circle. By the time the message came back to the beginning, it was totally different. No wonder that many of us are hearing confused messages.

Over the years while observing this proliferation of psychic phenomena, I have grown increasingly concerned.

This is because we really do have an amazing opportunity before us to ascend, to return home, to graduate from duality, to become Vibrantly Alive! The ascension is real. But since there is so much misinformation making the rounds, it is quite possible that the Greater Ascension will get lost and forgotten in the numerous levels of illusion which abound.

There is more than one level of ascension available to us at the present time.

Ascension is possible at many different levels of consciousness. It is of utmost importance that we are clear as to our ascension destination and that we make conscious choices as to where we want to go. Otherwise, we might discover that yes, we have ascended, but maybe not to where we thought we were going.

11:11

A Trigger of Remembrance:

For many years the numbers 11:11 have been mysteriously appearing to people all over the world. Often appearing on digital clocks, the sightings of 11:11 tend to occur during times of heightened awareness, having a most powerful effect on the people involved. This causes a reactivation of our cellular memory banks. There's a stirring deep inside, a hint of remembrance of something long forgotten. The appearance of 11:11 is also a powerful confirmation that we are on the right track, aligned with our highest Truth.

Throughout the years, I have personally encountered thousands of people all over the world who have experienced repeated sightings of 11:11. They all want to know what is happening to them and why. What does the 11:11 signify?

11:11 is a pre-encoded trigger placed into our cellular memory banks prior to our descent into matter which, when activated, signifies that our time of completion is near.

This refers to the completion of duality. When the 11:11 appears to you, it is your wake-up call. A direct channel opens up between you and the Invisible.

The 11:11 is an insertion point for the Greater Reality to enter into the present moment.

When this happens, it is time to stop whatever you are doing and Look Larger. A transfer is in position. You can enter the Greater Reality and seed your future and also, you can be seeded by the Invisible. You can ask for help in some specific area of your life or simply listen quietly and receive a revelation.

The appearance of 11:11 is an always beneficial act of Divine Intervention telling you that it is time to take a good look around you and see what is really happening. It's time to pierce the veils of illusion that keep us bound to an unreal world. You have been chosen, *because you are ready*, to step into the Greater Reality. To lead the way for others into a new way of living, into a Greater Love. To ascend from duality into Oneness.

The 11:11 is the bridge
between duality and Oneness.
It is our pathway into the Unknown.

On January 11, 1992 another great planetary activation took place called the 11:11. Once again, over a hundred thousand people participated around the world. The 11:11 was unique in that a series of Unified Movements was performed at three preordained times. The participants wore white to symbolize the purity of their inherent Oneness. Never before has such synchronized unity been achieved on Earth.

The purpose of this activation was to open the Doorway of the 11:11. This Doorway is the transition zone or bridge between two very different spirals of evolution, those of duality and Oneness. Each spiral is aligned with different Great Central Sun Systems. During the 11:11 Ceremony these two spirals overlapped and interlocked into a docking position. This Zone of Overlap is the actual Doorway of the 11:11. The overlapping of spirals remains in position until the 11:11 closes on December 31, 2011 when the two spirals of evolution will separate once again. Thus we have a twenty year period to graduate from duality and make our ascension into Oneness.

The 11:11 is but one, of several levels of ascension presently available to us. However, as far as I know, it is the one which will take us the greatest distance on our homeward journey and it will enable us to step free of the dimensional patterning of duality found within our present Great Central Sun System.

The Ascension is a process, not an event!

This means that if we really want to ascend, if we yearn to return Home, then we must, first of all, make the needed transformation within ourselves. It's not simply a matter of running around to the latest planetary activations, following the newest metaphysical trends, or listening to the flashiest New Age guru. These are all distractions from what is really going on. The ascension is a process, not an event.

The true ascension takes place within the core of our own beings and within the cells of our physical bodies. It's as real as that! We need to become whole beings, grounded in both the Earth and the Stars. We need to become Vibrantly Alive! We need to learn what Love really is and embody it as naturally as we breathe.

It's fine if you choose to make a conscious decision to remain in duality, or to be picked up by a spaceship, to ascend to the Fifth, Seventh or whatever Dimension, as long as you are *consciously* aware of your destination. There is no right or wrong way to ascend; there are simply different choices leading to different destinations. Perhaps, it is not for everyone at this time to make a quantum leap through the 11:11 into Oneness. But it's important that you are clear within yourselves as to what the differences in destination represent, so you can make the most appropriate choice.

Part of my function as a visionary is to explore and communicate our homeward journey through the Doorway of the 11:11. The 11:11 is not a stargate or another dimension; *it is a bridge of ascension into a new spiral of evolution anchored in Oneness.* I do not wish to criticize other levels of ascension, but rather to maintain clarity as to what the 11:11 is about, so it will not be buried in confusion as something which "happened in the past and is now complete."

The 11:11 is real and it is still in effect.

Our next step is to go through the Doorway of the 11:11 into the Invisible. *(And for the purpose of clarification, I would like to state that subsequent activations such as the one called "12:12" are entirely separate events belonging to an extremely different level of ascension. They have absolutely no connection with the 11:11.)* We have worked so hard to open the Doorway of the 11:11, *please*, let's not neglect our journey through it!

I know that each activation upon this planet, whether large or small, public or private, regardless of level of consciousness, serves to quicken our total awakening process and loosen the calcification of duality. I have deep gratitude to all who serve in this manner with full integrity. However, an alignment of focus is needed and an enlarged vision which acknowledges all parts of the Greater Map of Ascension.

The Eleven Gates

To make the shift from duality to Oneness we must travel in measured increments through ever more heightened bands of energy. This transfer of energy from duality into full Oneness cannot be achieved instantly; our duality-based beings would be unable to adjust to the accelerated energies and be fried to a crisp. This is why we have twenty years to pass through the 11:11. We will need all that time to recalibrate our beings so we can learn how to Live Large on a small planet.

Within the Doorway of the 11:11 there are Eleven Gates. Each Gate is a stepping up station to a new frequency band of energy. These gates are similar to locks in a canal. Once a Gate is activated and entered, we begin an intense process of transformation and initiation as our beings are immersed in a new frequency patterning. We then travel upon this frequency band of energy, mastering the lessons of the Gate until we reach the next Gate. Each Gate has an unique vibratory keynote with which we must align ourselves in a state of harmonic resonance. It is this process of alignment which gives us the necessary initiations and recalibrations to travel further.

The First Gate

Healing our Hearts:

The First Gate is entered as soon as we step inside the 11:11. We are leaving the old map and entering the mysterious, uncharted realms of the Unknown. Watery currents undulate all around us as the Invisible begins to reveal itself. The air feels like an aqueous substance. The focus here is on the healing of our emotions. This requires a constant process of letting go, a continuous reevaluation of our old ways of feeling, thinking and being. Many relationships are restructured or dissolved while we travel through the First Gate. With this healing of our hearts, we experience an activation of our One Heart, birthing our new emotional body.

Often during our passage through First Gate, we will meet someone who personifies our True Love. When this occurs, an immense feeling of a new, stronger Love floods through our beings, activated by our deep alignment of Essence, infusing us with sublime ecstasy and further recalibrating our emotional bodies. This can be almost overwhelming, for we are not used to such powerful Love. Many of these First Gate True Love relationships bring up so many unresolved issues lodged in our old emotional bodies that they never take root and flower. They merely show us the potential available for deeper Love and reveal the locations of our remaining hooks into duality. This adds yet more fuel to our transformation process, giving us excellent opportunities for facing and clearing whatever holds us back from healthy, empowered relationships.

The healing Presence of A•Qua•La A•Wa•La serves as our guide through these swirling waters of emotions. She is the Elohim of the Oceans and the Healer of Emotions and one of the last of such personified beings we shall encounter. She is joined by the dolphins who remind us to be playful on our journey, and by the whales who bring remembrance of what we have long forgotten. The whales are also the keepers of the long lost Phallus of Osiris which is finally returned to mankind. This will enable men to step into their true manhood and women to embrace their true womanhood, thus setting the stage for the entrance into the Second Gate.

The Second Gate

The Activation of Second Gate took place on June 5, 1993. Ceremonies were held all over the planet with the Master Cylinder located directly on the Equator inside the volcanic crater of Pululahua in Ecuador. While this was the date that the Second Gate was activated, it is important to remember that we are all on our own individual timetables of transformation.

Although a Gate cannot be entered until its activation, everyone doesn't enter it at the same time. Many are still passing through the First Gate, while others have yet to enter the 11:11. Our stretching out through the available open Gates is a natural occurrence, allowing us the needed time to transform and recalibrate our core beings. This passage cannot be rushed, forced or faked.

Second Gate represents the fusion of our deepest heart's desires with our highest spiritual goals. The fulfillment of our heart's desires becomes the next step on our spiritual path. The previous separation between the *personal* and the *spiritual* is hereby transcended.

And the two shall become One.

Isis and Osiris serve as the Gatekeepers of the Second Gate. This is their final act of service as separate beings, for in the act of holding open Second Gate, they become One Being. Their legend is brought to completion and they cease to exist as we have known them.

The keynote of the Second Gate is the two becoming One. This entails an intensive process of reunifying all our inherent polarities: inner male & female, Sun & Moon, Earth & Star. Our new emotional bodies are strengthened, further anchoring the One Heart. We now embody the Lovers from Beyond the Stars—a deeper, vaster Love than we ever experienced as True Loves. The reunion of *the Lovers from Beyond the Stars* back into One Being leads us to a heightened level of Love known as the Greater Love.

It is this newly birthed One Being, embodying the Greater Love, who is ready to step into our new futures anchored in the Invisible.

Our journey through the Second Gate will take over three years. By then, we will find that we have greatly transformed, far beyond what we can presently imagine. We will be experiencing totally new levels of Love. The changes inherent in the Second Gate are vaster than anything we have yet experienced. But it is important to remember that this is merely the beginning point. The rest of the journey has yet to be experienced and mapped.

• The Third Gate •

The Third Gate will be activated in 1997. Its keynote will be the establishment of the New Relationship patternings. These will be greatly expanded forms of partnerships, quite different than anything we have yet experienced. It will mark the loosening of exclusive relationships between two people. Where previously, "two is company, three is a crowd," now we can join together with unlimited numbers of people and form One Being. Our wholehearted expression of Love will no longer be limited, instead it will become All-Encompassing.

The activation of Third Gate will also give us the green light for the creation of conscious communities anchoring the Invisible into the physical, our Islands of Light.

Where

are

we?

This is the Map of the Invisible.

The black spiral is the path of duality.

Many of us now find ourselves

in the center of this spiral.

It is the completion of the old road.

•

We are on the brink of mastering duality.

•

This is why our futures

are no longer visible.

Why our best laid plans

do not come to fruition.

Why we no longer have

any vestige of control.

•

•

Nothingness

stands before us

at the end

of the old road.

•

•

Have our futures disappeared?

Where is our next step?

Everything is different here.

We are traveling on an entirely new map.

•

Now look again at the Map of the Invisible.

Look beyond duality's black spiral.

See the hidden spiral

in the Spaces-In-Between.

Notice that it is a much larger spiral.

And it has been there all along.

●

This is the Spiral of the Invisible.

It is anchored in ONENESS.

It is where we must travel.

●

•

Here we will find our futures,

our next step,

our Islands of Light,

and the relationships we have longed for

anchored in the Greater Love.

•

Something

is happening,

and it is

very,

very real.

Something is happening here,
and it's more real
than any of us can imagine.

This book is for all of us who know something profound is happening, and who are experiencing an unprecedented transformation of our Core Selves. It is a guidebook into the unexplored realms of the Invisible. It is an entry point into a new map and your passport to travel there.

Whatever path you took to reach this point no longer matters. It was merely your method of propulsion, the cosmic carrot which enticed you forward. Our journey thus far has given us the perfect experiences we needed to arrive here, NOW, poised at the entrance to the Unknown. Ready to jump off the old map, ready to leave behind all that we have known.

To travel deeper, get ready to let go of your old belief systems. Get ready to step free of the *Past That Never Was*. Get ready to go where few have gone before. . .

We are being woven into a New Matrix.

As we enter the Invisible, there is a loosening of the bonds which kept us tied into the Template of Duality. The threads of the old matrix begin to dissolve, setting us free from the old patterning. We are no longer bound by our previous definitions of Self, by old roles, conditioning and limitations. All boundaries have been erased. This is caused by the quickening within our Core Selves—heightened frequencies which no longer correspond to the sluggish vibrations of duality's matrix.

We have simply become too Large to fit into our previous existence.

At this point it is easier to perceive what isn't, rather than what is. A major portion of what was previously important to us has now become lifeless and unreal. Try as we may to proceed with our normal lives, we cannot. Something within us is indelibly transformed. We no longer fit into the old paradigm. Somewhat dismayed, we grasp onto our old security systems and discover that they give us no solace or protection. We dust off our well worn spiritual practices, but they take us nowhere new. We cling to our relationships and find them falling apart. We bring out our old tools, but they don't work. We grab our old concepts and philosophies, only to discover that they don't explain anything. We then focus on fulfilling our Divine Missions and not surprisingly, find that their time has passed.

A rising panic sets in. We now know all the things that we are not, but what are we? How can we be nothing? An all-pervading sense of emptiness surrounds us. Have we lost our way? Why does nothing work like it used to anymore?

What has happened to our vision, our certainty, our sense of control? Where is our clarity? We look around for outside help, searching for people, books or tools which will show us the way. There aren't any. . . We hold up our old map and can't find any familiar signposts.

We have traveled off the map of the known.

What do you do when you reach the end of the spiral of duality? When the road in front of you is a huge dead end? There is only one thing to do, leap off into the Unknown. Immerse yourself in the Invisible. And so you do. . .

Having made the leap, what we discover is yet more emptiness. We can't see anything! Our beings are stretched wide open and undefined. How uncomfortable! How awkward and uncertain. Perhaps, we should go back to the known. But then you try to go back and discover that you can't. You've become too big to fit into the old paradigm. What to do?

This is the time when you need to stop everything. Stop trying to think; stop struggling to see where you are. Turn to your heart and feel. Since you can't see anything, begin by carefully sensing the energies around you. Feel the undulating currents of the subtle energies. Ah. . . the air feels like water. Float in these subtle currents of the Invisible and feel how comforting it is. You are floating in liquid Love in the center of the One Heart.

Welcome to the Template of Oneness!

THE KEYS

TO THE

INVISIBLE

THE FIRST KEY:

Mastering the Art of Surfing

Mastering the Art of Surfing . . .

The Surf is up!

Surfing the subtle currents of the Invisible is similar to surfing the ocean waves. And it's a most useful skill at this point. First, let's learn how to study the condition of the surf. Since the subtle currents are continually changing, we need to constantly align ourselves with their movements. Try lying down and becoming very still until you can feel the undulating currents all around you. If you are very quiet, you should also be able to feel the watery currents slowly shifting inside your body. Now, let the subtle currents both inside and outside you flow together in unison. This will align you more deeply with the Invisible.

What is the surf of the subtle currents doing? How would you describe it? Is it calm or wild, choppy or stagnant? Get to know your surf so that at any given moment you can accurately read it. This is especially helpful upon awakening in the morning. It will tell you much about the energies of the day. The next step is to align yourself with the surf. This is very important if you want to flow through your day, working *with* the inherent energies, rather than against them. *Here are some examples:*

• Calm Surf •

A good day for steadily pacing yourself, accomplishing things in a peaceful manner. A serene day filled with positive energy and Love.

• Wild Surf •

There are many variations within this category. If you properly align yourself with Wild Surf, you can accomplish much. It will give you lots of passion, energy and momentum. It is a time of clear, decisive action without effort or struggle.

• Battering Surf •

This is a rough surf. Be very gentle with yourself and others. Keep as quiet as possible until it changes. Avoid confrontations. It's definitely not the kind of day to go out and press your luck. Instead, stay home and read. Make yourself as cozy as possible.

• Choppy Surf •

An unpredictable surf which can go in any direction. Your mind will be full of wild, uncontrollable thoughts, most of which have no basis in reality. Avoid decisions since you are not coming from a place of clarity. Try to be extra alert and grounded, otherwise you can have minor accidents. The best thing to do in Choppy Surf is the small practicalities of life. A good day to tidy the house, do your laundry, work in the garden; any unchallenging physical activities which give your wayward mind something to focus on. Once you do this, the crazy energies will balance out and Choppy Surf will change into something else.

• Splashing Surf •

A challenging, emotional surf. It will bring out a spectrum of surface emotions. One minute you will be happy–then sad–then angry. None of these emotions are very deep or enduring, so just let them pass through you. It's difficult to find a way to align yourself with a Splashing Surf, but once you do, your emotions will smooth out. One thing that will help is to remember that these emotions are not based on anything personal. You are simply experiencing some of the collective planetary emotions for the purpose of transmutation.

• Still Surf •

Still Surf is surf with little or no movement. When you feel becalmed in Still Surf, don't force yourself into action. Stay as quiet as possible. Retreat. Go within. It is an excellent time to access the depths of your being. Also a good time for study or research. If you have to go into the world or interact with people, remain as quiet as possible. It is not an easy time to get anything done on a physical level. If you have to work, you'll have the greatest success if you do things slowly and thoroughly.

• The Doldrums •

While this isn't officially a surf, it is something which you might encounter while surfing. Physically, the Doldrums is an area near the Equator in the Pacific Ocean where sailing ships often become becalmed, sometimes for months. It is a place of little or no wind. The Doldrums differ from Still Surf in their sense of an all-pervading heaviness. When we enter the Doldrums, nothing seems to work in our lives. Everything is weighted down. The surf has disappeared. When this happens, it's time to make a change. Do something radical—like change yourself, let go of some long held belief, or simply make a massive surrender. That should set you free from the Doldrums and push you into an exciting breakthrough.

• Riptide Surf •

This is surf which appears calm, but contains hidden pockets of danger or whirlpools which can suddenly catapult you to a totally different place. We often initially read this as Calm Surf until we are surprised by a dramatic, unexpected turn of events. As we become Master Surfers, we will learn to discern Riptide Surf before it pulls us in.

• Swooning Surf •

Swooning Surf is filled with concentrated Love energies. That's Ecstatic Love energies. Heightened Ecstatic Love energies. When Swooning Surf is up, you don't need to eat or sleep and are definitely unpinned from time and space. A magical time when miracles can be achieved. Love is in the air and melts everyone it encounters. Need we say more?

• Quantum Surf •

This is the special surf which is aligned with the waves of the Celestial Seas. It brings forth the really BIG WAVES. Huge, undeniable waves... When Quantum Surf is around, jump on your surfboards and ride the Beam! This is the surf of quantum leaps, major breakthroughs and achieving the impossible. So when Quantum Surf is up, drop everything else and ride these waves as far as you can.

When the tide rolls in, ride the waves.
When the tide is out, collect shells.

Once you have recognized the condition of the surf, you can begin your day with maximum effectiveness. However, it's important to remember that the surf can change anytime. Program yourself to check out the subtle currents on a regular basis throughout the day and realign yourself to them if they have changed.

As you develop greater familiarity and mastery with the prevailing surf, you will learn how to smooth out the rough spots in your life by working with the subtle currents of the Invisible. And by learning to feel the subtle currents and aligning yourself to them, you have received your First Key to the Invisible.

Carefully Choosing Your Breaks.

In ocean surfing it's important to watch where the waves are breaking, then choose which wave you are going to surf. If you choose the wave closest to shore, it will be the easiest wave and the tamest, but it will lead you right back to where you started. If you choose the second break, it will be larger and will take you further. And if you go for the third wave, you will have to swim out quite a distance from the safety of shore. It will be the wildest wave and will take you the furthest.

The same is true with the subtle currents of the Invisible. If you don't go for it with your full commitment, then surely, you will quickly return back to where you started. But you need to be careful with that third wave, for if you go out too far you run the risk of capsizing and being swept out to sea. Learn the waves and choose which one you ride with wisdom and discernment.

- Keep your commitment to go the distance firm and unwavering.

- Always be prepared to stretch your envelope and go past your comfort zone.

- As soon as you have done this, integrate your experience and reground yourself.

• Surf Rules! •

What this means is that once we're in the Invisible we lose our old sense of control. It's not just a matter of letting go of control, we simply don't have any. Although it's debatable if we ever did. But, at least, we thought we did. Now we definitely don't have any vestige of control. We have been thrust into a totally new place which we cannot see, way beyond our previous experiences or known boundaries. All we can do is feel the surf and align ourselves with the prevailing currents. Hence, *Surf Rules!*

At this point, we would do well to simply yield to the waves and let them take us where they wish. Since we don't really know where we want to go and can't see where we are anyway. Personally, I have developed a strong trust and respect for the waves of the Invisible. They have never led me astray or to anywhere I didn't want to go. My only problems have come about when I was not aligned to them. *Surf Rules!*

• The Overlapping of Realities •

Since the 11:11 Activation in 1992, there has been an overlay of simultaneous reality systems on Earth. It's like living in several different worlds at once. Although this can be confusing at times, it also can make life more fun. Learn to surf these overlapping worlds and different dimensions. It may sometimes be wild, but it will never be boring!

If you are Large enough, your being will be able to straddle multiple waves of realities, and simultaneously interact with all of them. However, it's important to keep your being anchored in Oneness at all times, so you don't get drawn into smaller worlds.

Stay Large and Surf Wild!

THE SECOND KEY:

To See Is To Be

To See Is To Be. . .

Here we are, somewhat gracefully surfing the waves of the Invisible. . .

Our next step is to develop new ways of seeing so that we can see into the Unseen.

Everything is different on the new map.

This means that we can pretty well let go of all ways of seeing which used to work for us on the old template. In the New Matrix everything is interwoven together in the One Heart. There is no more separation. Seeing has become a *seeing/feeling*. This is a sensing with our full being of the interconnectedness of everything around us.

In order to see into the Invisible, we will first take an introductory journey through the various levels of seeing which are presently available. Please try to experience each level of seeing in your physical body as we travel along. Here are some of the stops along the path:

• A Seeing Chart •

Template of Duality

Physical Eyes:

This is the first level of seeing which we are taught from birth as being the only method of seeing. When we look through our physical eyes, we focus on the physical world. This is a great way of seeing to use when you want to see separate objects on the physical plane. The physical detail is heightened and the surrounding energy is diffused.

Third Eye:

Aha, we have discovered that we have chakras! The third eye is located in the center of our forehead. It is a very important psychic energy center within the Spirituality of Duality. Once we activate our third eyes, we can see beyond the physical. A whole new world opens up. We can see auras, past lives, disease, karmic patterns and a host of other strange stuff located in the astral plane and the Fourth Dimension. When we are using our third eyes, the physical plane somewhat blurs out as the surrounding and underlying energy patterns begin to emerge.

Triangulation:

When we blend the seeing of our physical eyes with our third eye, their energies triangulate, forming a new unit. This triangle of merged physical and psychic energy has enhanced seeing capabilities. You can try this by forming a triangle with your hands and placing the apex over your third eye. Now look out with your new seeing unit and feel the difference.

The All-Seeing Eye of AN:

This is the apex point of seeing within the Template of Duality. As it is located within the Zone of Overlap bridging the two, *very different,* spirals of evolution, it also serves as the foundation or entry point into new ways of seeing. It's the jumping off point into the Unseen.

Here's how to arrive at the All-Seeing Eye. *As you do this, please concentrate on the shifts in your energy rather than your arm movements.* Stand up straight with your arms at your sides, looking outwards. Now very slowly raise your arms until the inside of your left palm is flat on the top of your head. Your left elbow should be extended out to your left side. At the same time, raise your right arm and place the palm of your right hand on top of your left hand, with your right elbow pointing outwards to your right side. When you look at yourself in a mirror, you should be forming one large eye with your head located in the center of this new eye.

As you repeat this process, feel the immense shift in energy as it rises upwards. Now look outwards through your larger eye. This is the All-Seeing Eye of AN. The reason AN is mentioned here is that this process entails unifying your inner polarities of Sun & Moon into One Being.

When you are using your All-Seeing Eye, you have a much greater vantage point than before. You are seeing from a vaster, more all-encompassing clarity, blending and utilizing all other previous methods of seeing into a heightened vision.

You might also try this practice with another person. Stand facing each other and open into the All-Seeing Eye. You will immediately align into One Mind. Now slowly turn and face outwards. You will feel that you are the two eyes of one vaster being. Return to facing each other and feel that Oneness intensify.

This process can also be done with a group of people standing in a circle. It is one of the fastest methods I know of for aligning a group of strangers into Oneness.

Template of Oneness

The One Eye:

Now we are ready to step into an infinitely vaster level of seeing. As you master the One Eye, you will be able to see into the Invisible. Please remember that this is a *seeing-feeling*, a sense of being interwoven into Oneness. You will *see-feel* everything around you as part of your vaster Self. Often you will be able to see things behind you and on the other side of physical barriers, such as walls.

Stand in the All-Seeing Eye position and look out through your large eye. Now very slowly raise your hands off your head, bringing them upwards, outwards and downwards, until they come to rest at your sides. While you are doing this, keep looking outwards. Feel your All-Seeing Eye expand as it opens outwards. Now you are seeing with your whole body as well as with all the space around you. Keep practicing this until it becomes your New Normal way of seeing.

THE THIRD KEY:

I Am
That
I Am Not

I Am That I Am Not. . .

*Seeing with One Eye, we can feel
our interconnectedness with everything.*

This is a good beginning; but what do we do now? Who are we? Where are we going? How are we going to get there?

The Third Key is to stay open and undefined. Accept the Unacceptable. Accept that you are in a new place without any maps. Don't try to know anything. Don't try to do anything. Don't try to make anything happen. And especially, don't be in a hurry to discover who you are. Remain open and undefined, without labels, without boundaries. Take heart that if you no longer know who you are, you must be doing quite well! This is one of the definitions of enlightenment. If you need to know something, look at all the things which you are not. They should be quite clear to you by now.

This is an excellent time to take a good, penetrating look around you and start clearing out the clutter. Get rid of those clothes which you're never going to wear again, which don't resonate with your True Self. Do you really need all those books that you've already read? Those old letters? Go through everything and strip away the meaningless debris. Sell or give away everything you no longer need. At this point it's better to be empty and true to yourself, then surrounded by the clutter of the past.

Start cleaning out your life in the same manner. How do you clutter your days? What meaningless activities can be dropped? Get rid of all obligations in your life which are based on guilt, old patterns, or which you do because you're *supposed to*. Strip away and hone your life until it is real, unvarnished, without compromise. This includes friends who no longer share similar interests and relationships which are unsupportive or lifeless. Go ahead, be ruthless and unrelenting. It will feel great to clear out the entanglements which keep you ensnared in duality.

Next, you can begin releasing your old judgments and assumptions. They were all based on an old reality system which we are leaving behind. Don't allow yourself to be limited in this way anymore. Then wrap yourself in a blanket of forgiveness. Forgive everyone who has ever hurt you; forgive all your past experiences, and most importantly, FORGIVE YOURSELF.

Learn to speak when you have something to say and to be quiet when you don't. Purge away all those platitudes, those things you say that aren't really true. Be real when you communicate. Small talk and mindless chatter simply clutter the mind and thicken your energy. Don't keep yourself in a constant state of distraction with socializing, television, gossip, magazines, watching sports, worrying about politics, etc. Give yourself lots of free time to be open, empty and quiet. This is when you're going to deepen your being and most feel the Invisible. Spend as much time as you can out in nature. Contemplating the shifting weather patterns, the sky, trees, mountains, and the behavior of wildlife, will bring wondrous revelations.

No-Mind is always preferable to 3D mind.

Don't be afraid to not know. You don't have to pretend to be all-knowing all the time. None of us have all the answers anymore. I don't know of anyone on the planet who does. Usually if they think they do, then they simply haven't gone far enough into the Invisible. The old traditional gurus might have all the answers within the Spirituality of Duality, but most of them have not gone beyond the state of enlightenment, which isn't as evolved as we originally perceived. It used to be that if we had the questions, we could access the answers. Now we don't even have enough criteria to ask the right questions.

Don't forget that we're entering the unexplored territory of the great Unknown. And guess why it's called the Unknown? Because at this point, it's not knowable. So it's all right and quite appropriate not to know who we are, where we are, and where we're going. It's actually quite refreshing to let go of our old storehouses of dusty knowledge. If like many of us, your memory is starting to fade, then let it go. We need to forget most of what we learned anyway. In your new state of No-Mind, turn from *knowing* to *feeling*. Think with your heart—the One Heart. Allow your purest, Truest Love to lead you through each day.

No-Mind is a state of alert emptiness.

When we are in a state of No-Mind, we are more open to the One. All things can be accessed in their appropriate timing. Being empty frees us to be truly responsive. It frees us to feel and to know. It's similar to the information revolution which is taking place right now through computers and the Internet. With computers we now have access to unlimited amounts of information. We can talk to anyone all over the world. We can browse through the world's greatest libraries; view distant art collections, get the latest earthquake data, gather information on any subject. We no longer have to carry around with us cumbersome encyclopedias and reference works. It's all floating on the nebulous Internet, an invisible world that doesn't exist on the physical, but can be accessed from the physical.

This is the same thing that happens to us when we enter No-Mind. We all have direct, immediate access to the whole of the One. This world also emanates from the Invisible, yet can, *and must*, be brought into the physical until both realms have been totally, irrevocably, merged into Oneness.

No-Mind is good. Emptying out the clutter in your mind is tremendously freeing. So what! if you can't remember all those phone numbers anymore, or the names of distant acquaintances. Let the past slip away. Let your own personal history disappear. It will only serve you to become more of your True Self.

- If you don't like what you've been or done in your lifetime, then the way to be free of your past is to so change yourself that you are no longer the same person as before.

- Accept what you have been and what you are not.

- We can all be the Great Beings that we inherently are.

- We can all live the fulfilling lives we would like to live.

- Simply BE REAL *no matter what,* and plunge into Living Large!

THE FOURTH KEY:

No News
Is
Good News

No News Is Good News. . .

Now, let's unplug ourselves from the media.

Let the world get along by itself for awhile. It's nice to stay informed and all that, but most of what is labeled *The News* is not real. It is *The News* of the Template of Duality. This doesn't mean that it's not happening. Of course it is, but is it really important? Does it have any enduring relevance to us?

Take a good look at the subtle manipulation done by our third dimensional media. How there is always the *crisis of the moment* to keep us distracted from seeing what is truly real. Duality is extremely clever. Clever enough to create a continual state of crisis in shifting places around the world, constantly amplified by a voracious media to keep us focused away from ourselves, away from what is really going on.

Something is happening, and it more real than any of us can imagine.

What's truly funny is that something momentous is happening, and it's so real that the media can't see it. Here it is, the biggest story of all time, and it goes unreported. If you're continually focused on this and that media event, the latest celebrity scandal, the scattered wars of duality, the deceitful maneuverings of selfish politicians, and the shifting state of a false world economy, you just might miss the greater story. And this greater story is why we are here and what gives our lives meaning.

We're creating the Real News just by being.

If you want to be connected with the Real News, then don't get hooked into the smaller news as projected by the established media operating within the framework of duality, but look at yourselves. The same is also true of most of the *New Age* media, because much of what they report is illusory as well.

Here's the Big Story that's largely unreported:

A significant segment of the world population is in the process of unhooking themselves from duality. We are significant because we are the more aware beings, the ones who consciously serve our Higher Purpose, the true spiritual leaders and courageous explorers into the Unknown. What will happen when we have mastered duality and stepped into Oneness? How will the Earth be transformed when the Invisible anchors into the physical? *Now these are interesting stories. . .* And of course, the media is missing it completely.

So is the story of the 11:11 which is probably the biggest thing to happen on Earth in recent times, maybe ever. How often do we come together at various spots around the planet and do a series of Unified Movements at synchronized times to interlock two different spirals of evolution? This story is so huge that most of us haven't yet come close to understanding it. That includes those who actually participated in the 11:11 Activation and still think that we anchored the Fourth Dimension! It is so infinitely vaster than that. But how many of us really care to know the truth? Isn't it just a lot easier to keep distracted, running from one spiritual activity to the next, without really understanding what it's all about, without making the necessary changes within ourselves.

If we want to live it, first we must become it.

Obvious, isn't it? If you want to experience real Love, then first we must embody Love. If we want to live in the New, then our very cells must be recalibrated to the higher frequencies of the Greater Reality. We must become New Beings by birthing our True Selves. *We are the Real News; we're the most exciting story there is.*

Learn to look • b e y o n d • the current events.

If you still want to stay hooked into the media of duality, then it's important that you develop the ability to *look beyond* the news. Read those newspapers and watch television, but always keep looking *beyond* the presented facts. Watch the ebb and flow of the prevailing energy currents. What is really happening? Keep yourself anchored in a wider vantage point. Look at everything from a vaster perspective. What is the essence behind this story? See it all as the play of duality and don't allow yourself to get drawn into the drama. Otherwise, duality will hook you and reel you back into a narrow perspective, into fears for survival, into its numerous illusions. Calmly observe the happenings of this planet from a stance of openness, expanded Love and freedom. We can be of greatest service by maintaining our anchoring in Oneness.

THE FIFTH KEY:

Mastering Surrender

Mastering Surrender. . .

Surrender is the clue to arrive at something New.

Our next step is to Master the Art of Surrendering. As much as we might sometimes prefer, surrendering simply cannot be avoided. It is a continual process along our journey. We do have a small choice in the matter. This choice is not whether we shall surrender or not, but whether we choose to surrender gracefully or have what we are so tenaciously holding onto, ripped away from us. Having repeatedly experienced both methods, I strongly recommend the graceful surrender.

How can we tell when it is time to surrender? The clues are all around us and not subtle at all. First there's a sense of heaviness or compression which settles into our life. It feels like we are bogged down in thick mud. Our life experiences feel stagnant and joyless. We have become petrified by our outmoded attitudes and habits. Nothing works easily anymore.

Then comes a subtle whisper trying to get our attention. Unless we are already Masters of Surrender, this first hint is usually shrugged off as the workings of an overactive imagination. Besides, we're too busy or too attached to what we know has to be changed or let go of.

Next comes the *tap, tap, tap* on the shoulder. It's undeniable. We now know that surrender is calling us. Yet all too often, we choose to ignore this call, thinking that perhaps it will go away if we don't respond. *Wishful thinking.* Surrender is far more stubborn than any of us. If we *still* don't listen, the next step will be the large thud or sudden shock in our lives when change is forcibly imposed upon us. *"How can life be so cruel? What have I done to deserve this?"* we lament, feeling so undeserving of this harsh twist of fate.

All of this could have been avoided if we had just Mastered the Art of Surrender in the first place. But there's a secret to successful surrendering which shall now be revealed. If you understand it, *if you make this truth your own,* then you never need fear surrendering again.

> You can safely surrender anything,
> • everything •
> without fear
> because anything which resonates
> with your Highest Truth will remain.

As the ancient Chinese proverb states, "If it's really your horse, you can let it go." What truly belongs to you cannot be lost. *Our only fears are of losing what no longer resonates with our Highest Truth.* And we might ask ourselves, why do we want to keep those things which hold us back from embodying our True Self?

The other truth about surrender is that when you do it, it must be real. You simply cannot fake surrender. Nor can you make a deal with surrender. Such as, "I'll let go of this, if I can keep that." I know this because I've tried and it doesn't work. Surrender knows if you are doing it with your 100% commitment or if you're trying to hide something behind your back. So don't even bother to attempt to fake it. If you're going to surrender, give it everything you've got.

Surrender is the door
   to arrive at something more.

The joy of surrendering comes after it is accomplished. There's such an amazing sense of lightness and release. It's so tremendously liberating! A pathway opens up before you and wondrous new things come into your life. They were probably just waiting around until there was enough clear space to enter. Surrendering is easy and fun once you get the hang of it. It doesn't even take courage; just trust in yourself and in the waves of the Invisible.

• A Practice to Master Surrendering •

Let's begin by creating a huge symbolic bonfire in the center of your room. We stress the word *symbolic* here; you don't need to set your house on fire. These are the Fires of Purification and Renewal. It will sear away anything which doesn't resonate with your Highest Truth, so treat your bonfire with respect. We're going to make this bonfire by bringing down a shaft of the Greater Central Sun. Simply reach up and grab a shaft of light and pull it down. It's as easy as that. Now anchor this shaft of Light into the Earthstar in the center of the planet, just to make it nice and stable. After doing this, you should have a brilliantly glowing bonfire.

• Bonfire One •
Pass it on!

For our first bonfire, we going to make a pile of all those things which we no longer need. Put in it not only your outdated possessions, but all your unsupportive relationships, old attitudes, ingrained habits, and self imposed limitations. Be thorough as you comb through your being. This is your big opportunity to really clean the closets of your life and your being. Create a mountain of old philosophies, spiritual practices, belief systems, fears, doubts, compromises, etc.

When you are done, visualize all the items in your huge pile being given to the people and places where it will best serve. If anything is left over, lovingly place it in the bonfire. Feel how much lighter you've become...

• Bonfire Two •
Completing the old, frees me for the New!

We're going to start a new pile in which we're going to place everything that we need to complete. This can include family obligations, unresolved relationship issues, education or job training, business projects, selling property, financial debts, etc. Anything which keeps you from fully stepping into living your Highest Truth.

Now visualize all the items in this pile being effortlessly brought to completion. See yourself stepping forward into greater freedom...

• Bonfire Three •
Melt those broken hearts!

This is the pile of old template love. Put into it all your broken hearts as well as all the hearts you have broken. Your disappointments, deep sorrows of the heart, unrequited loves, betrayals and those deep-rooted abandonment issues. Dig deep into your emotional body and place all those hidden old hurts onto your pile. Forgive everyone who has ever hurt you and most importantly, forgive yourself.

Pick up this mountain of painful, old emotions and with deep gratitude for all it has taught you, place it in the center of the bonfire. Your heart has now been cleansed and made ready for activating the One Heart. . .

• Bonfire Four •
Dissolve old definitions!

The next pile is composed of all the vows we have made since we first incarnated as individual selves. Place in it all your old roles: as mother, father, brother, sister, child, husband, wife, lover, teacher, healer, business-person, Angel, star commander etc. Add any religious affiliations you may have picked up along your journey. You might as well throw in your Divine Missions for good measure. Oh, and here's another good one. Toss in your personal power. I know that it took you a long time to get it, but we really don't need it anymore. Personal power is very limiting and keeps us from accessing true power which is actually no-power, and is available in abundance for all.

This is the pile that usually brings up the most resistance. If it does, then look at those things which you hesitate to surrender. It will tell you a lot about yourself, including where some of your hooks into duality are located. If you can't willingly surrender everything right now, then remember what you are holding onto and wait until the right moment, *hopefully soon*, to let them go.

Now pick up this mountain of roles, vows, responsibilities, power and missions and place them into the bonfire. Add some marshmallows if you like, and watch it all burn to a delightful crisp. Do you feel lighter yet?

• Bonfire Five •
My favorite things!

This is a tricky one. Put into this pile everything which you would like to keep. This includes all the qualities of yourself which you most like, plus your finest skills and aptitudes, spiritual beliefs, healthy relationships, your career, family and favorite animals. You can also include possessions like your house, car, computer, paintings, crystals, stereos and clothes—whatever you have which you would like to keep.

Make sure you include your name. You might be surprised how attached many people are to their names. Have you ever noticed how many people name things after themselves? Or how important it is to get credit for something you did? Toss in all your names and titles.

What a beautiful pile you have created. This is the best of you and your life. You can admire it for a few minutes if you like, then lovingly place all of it into the bonfire! There it goes. . .

• Bonfire Six •
Betting the ranch!

At this point you might think that there's nothing left to get rid of, but there is. You forgot yourself. If we're going to surrender, we may as well do the full surrender, so let's step into the bonfire. Get up and walk right into it and feel yourself seared to the core. Then let your core burn away. *Going, going, gone...*

Nothing is more than something.

Slowly the fire burns out. As it does, allow yourself the luxury of being nothing, having nothing. Do not be in a hurry to redefine yourself or reassume old roles. Keep open, *wide open* and free. Remain like this for as long as possible. Don't go running around searching to see what survived the bonfire. Wait until it comes to you. Watch yourself so you don't fall into old attitudes and assumptions. Stay New. The best is yet to come...

THE SIXTH KEY:

The Filters of Duality

The Filters of Duality. . .

Everything we have experienced on Earth until now has been seen through the filters of duality.

All of our perceptions have been clouded by illusion. This includes what we see with our physical eyes to our highest spiritual truths. We have been living our lives, making our decisions, creating our relationships, following our goals, under a diminished reality system and lesser truth.

It's like sitting at a small table and putting our full concentration on the objects resting on the table. Earnestly, we move around the pieces on the table, trying to put them into pleasing patterns. Trying to create meaning from the meaningless. Giving the small objects so much of our focused attention that we fail to realize how big we really are. Remember when we were children and played with toy cars or dolls; it's much the same as that. Even back then, we were always so much larger than the worlds which we created.

Well, it's time to look around us, time for an uplifting reality check. You might begin by noticing that you are not a small object on the table. In fact, you are much *larger* than the table. Not only are you larger, but you have the ability to move the objects on the table to wherever you want. You can even remove them or add new ones! Maybe, we're not as inconsequential and powerless as we thought.

Now look up from the table for a minute. *My, my,* what do you see? That there's more to existence than this table which has held your attention for so long. The table is located in a room and this space is VAST compared to the table. Gaze about at the room you are in, then look back at the table. See how small it is compared to where you really are. You have just made a quantum leap to another reality system.

Now let's exercise our newly discovered freedom. Get up from your chair. You can leave the table by itself. Nothing on it is going anywhere without you. It needs you to give it life. Without your attention it becomes static and unmoving. The same is true of duality. The only reason it exists is because we give it life by believing in it. And we can only live in duality by making ourselves smaller than we are.

While we're at it, let's go into another room. Here's another universe waiting to be discovered. Now we're getting pretty good at exploring our multidimensional realities. Your home is a fairly accurate map of the numerous reality systems available to us at any given moment. And as you see, it's not difficult to travel between the worlds.

If you're ready for another quantum leap, please step outside into the immeasurable vastness of nature. What awesome complexity! Nature is full of maps, large and small, which you can explore whenever you wish. Now remember the table. How important it was, how caught up you were in what you were doing there. How it all felt so real at the time.

There are worlds within worlds waiting to be explored.

These worlds can be found both inside and outside you. They are always available. To find them you must loosen your attention on smaller reality systems, open your being, and go explore the Unknown.

It's always our choice as to which reality system we're going to live our life in. We are inherently vast beings, capable of living in myriad simultaneous realities or the Greater Reality itself. How sad that so many people remain locked into the confines of duality. Letting their fears of the Unknown dictate their limited parameters. Of course, once you get a taste of the vastness which is available, it becomes increasingly difficult to remain small. And with repeated immersions into the heady, exhilarating Template of Oneness, we grow so Large that, try as we may, we don't fit back into our narrow, old worlds.

The filters of duality heighten the illusion of separation.

The physical world is not yet an accurate mirror of the Greater Reality. This realization is important if you wish to remove the filters of duality and see things as they really are. Since we were born into a reality system based on duality, practically everything that we were taught is backwards.

For example:

Are we really physical beings having spiritual experiences, or is it the other way around?
We are both physical & spiritual beings. Each is equally important and each is a part of our vaster One Being. Our task is to focus on embodying that One Being.

It's scary to be vast and safer to be small.
It's actually far more frightening and uncomfortable to be fragments of our True Selves. There is nothing safer than to be consciously woven into the One.

Is death really the end of our existence?
Birth and death are simply transition points or doorways into and out of physical form. Our True Self is eternal. Dying is similar to going to sleep at night, and in the morning we are reborn.

Is God a being separate from us?
The concept of God as a personification of the One, *separate from us,* is a distortion caused by the filters of duality. In the Template of Oneness, nothing is separate from the One.

Have we ever left Home?
Of course not! We just have to become Large enough to see where we are. When we do, it will be found all around us, *right here, right now.*

Do physical beings have individual souls?
Only in the Template of Duality. When we are woven into Oneness, we are part of a deeper harmonic, a new Matrix. Our Selves still carry a unique perspective or patterning based on their present vantage point within the wholeness of the One, but the soul envelope which keeps us separate dissolves.

What's the difference between a tree and a wild goose?
Very little, actually. Let me explain this with a story: A few years ago I was visiting a bird refuge in New Mexico. It was late afternoon and we stopped by a lake to watch the sunset. As I gazed at the lake, I saw the usual things—trees on the shore reflected in the lake, geese flying overhead, clouds in the sky. Then something quite magical and unexpected happened; the filters of duality started dissolving. Suddenly, the entire scene before me was transformed. It was as if I was seeing for the first time. Filled with wonder, I began laughing from the sheer joy of finally seeing clearly. Everything had been turned inside out.

We've been programmed that everything in this world has a separate identity: a tree is a tree, a cloud is a cloud. But now I saw that the reflection in the lake was truer than looking at the individual objects. The waters of the lake represented the One Heart. In the still surface of the lake I now saw the trees-of-the-One, the birds-and-clouds-of-the-One. Everything was part of this Greater Oneness.

Everything is woven together in the One Heart. All of our beings send forth luminous, fibrous strands of Love which expand outwards until we encounter another lifestream. Then our strands weave together with the so-called others, forming radiant mandalas of Light. This patterning is a small part of the Hologram of Wholeness. It all vibrates in accord with the harmonic resonance of the New Matrix. And even this New Matrix isn't really new, it's been there all along, only it couldn't be perceived as long as we were looking through the filters of duality.

• Dissolving the filters of duality •

Each day is the beginning of new life; we are reborn anew. It's important to remember this and to act upon it. We must let go of all our previous assumptions and begin with a clean slate. Continually look at everything with new eyes. See it as if for the first time.

When you get up out of bed, don't just rush to the kitchen and prepare what you usually eat. Go to the kitchen as if you have never been there before and see what your body wants to eat today. It may be the usual fare, or it might be something quite different. Meet each situation and every person with heightened openness and love.

Be open to Change.

Watch all your responses to the situations around you. Are you responding unconsciously in your old, accustomed manner, or are you meeting each situation with new eyes? This is especially challenging in the area of relationships. It's very easy here to fall into our pre-established limiting roles and patterns; and it's essential that we do not.

Relationships can keep us hooked into duality like nothing else. Even if you're in a karmic relationship with a partner anchored in duality, *you* don't need to respond in the old ways. Do the GO practice and anchor your being in Oneness. Now respond in a new way.

There is never more than One.

Most importantly, keep a larger perspective on everything.
DARE TO BE LARGE! Large beings interact with the world
from a vaster vantage point. Large beings feel their interconnectedness with the Greater Oneness and ground this
into their everyday lives. They courageously claim their
freedom from the confines of the small, limited world of
duality. As you do this, the filters of duality shall increasingly dissolve.

THE SEVENTH KEY:

Ready, Set, GO!

Ready, Set, GO!...

As we travel deeper into the Invisible, it is essential that we keep our beings well grounded.

To do this, we have created a practice called the GO that will give you the needed balance to assimilate the heightened energies of the Template of Oneness. You should do the GO every time you stand up until it becomes automatic. This will be your new everyday stance which will help you meet each situation in life with grace, empowerment and balance. The GO has three parts. Each part is important and should not be omitted. It's also essential that you do the GO in the proper order.

• Part One •
Anchoring the Earthstar

Stand up and send your energy downwards into the Earthstar located in the core of the planet. When you reach the Earthstar, you will feel an interlocking into position. If you don't feel this, you need to go deeper. This extends your energy into the Earth and gives you the necessary grounding.

• Part Two •
Bringing in the Beam

Reach upwards to the Greater Central Sun and bring down a shaft of Light. Send this down through your being into the Earth and anchor it into the Earthstar. This transforms you into a Pillar of Light. Feel the strength this gives you, the deep sense of connectedness between Earth and Star.

• Part Three •
Activating the One Heart

Place your hands together in the prayer position, palms together, fingertips pointing upwards. Put your hands in front of your heart. Now squeeze them together tightly, pushing out all your broken hearts, all the hearts you've broken, all your emotional disappointments, all the distortions of love which you have experienced throughout your cycle of embodiments. Let go of jealousy, possessiveness, betrayal, & abandonment. Keep pushing your hands together until only the purest Essence of True Love remains.

Now slowly open your hands, stretching out the Essence of True Love. Do this very consciously and carefully. If you lose your focus, simply start again. While you are expanding your Essence of True Love, move out past your previous comfort zone, stretching your hands out beyond your body. When you have fully expanded your True Love, turn your palms so they face outwards. Feel your heart, feel with the openness of your One Heart. Notice how much larger and cleaner your Love has become!

• The Sitting GO •

The GO can also be done in a sitting position. This is an excellent way to sit when you are working with powerful energies. It's the position I use when I am giving workshops. It keeps you balanced and grounded. Make sure that your feet are placed directly on the floor and that your legs are uncrossed. Now place your hands palms down upon your legs and feel how this anchors your beings.

The GO is our new stance
which helps us integrate
the Invisible with the physical.

It should be practiced repeatedly until we automatically do it each time we stand up. When you master the energies of the GO, you will no longer need to move your arms; the expanding and balancing of your energy will happen naturally. This is known as the Subtle GO.

THE MASTER KEY:

Sacred Union

Sacred Union. . .

The Master Key to our entire evolutionary journey is Sacred Union.

Both our spiritual evolutionary journey of embodying our vastness and our biological journey as we evolved from single celled creatures to the human forms we inhabit today derive from the primal impulse to experience ever greater depths of Sacred Union.

The sense of abandonment and pain of separation which we've experienced since our initial separation from *conscious* Oneness when we descended into matter has created an undeniable yearning for unobstructed, perfect union. This deep yearning serves as our main method of propulsion on our long journey of reawakening and reclaiming our wholeness.

Sacred Union is the conscious merger back into Oneness.

It is this deep, unrequited yearning which has led us on our search for the perfect partner, *our True Love,* or as Plato says, our *Split Apart*. This other part of ourself is really our Lover from Beyond the Stars. Together we become the personification of the unified One Heart. At the core of our longing for Sacred Union with a partner is the even deeper yearning for *conscious,* eternal union with the One. This is what has sparked our enduring commitment to the Homeward Journey. Always, the Call to Sacred Union leads us forward into greater wholeness and Oneness.

Whatever paths we have chosen to take,
   whatever choices we make,
      (conscious or unconscious),
  our goal is Sacred Union.

Sacred Union is where we will find true fulfillment and wholeness. The entire journey of remembrance, reclaiming the many forgotten fragments of our beings, merging small selves into our Vaster Selves, is the journey of Sacred Union. Unifying our inner male & female polarities, uniting Sun & Moon, merging Earth & Star, physical & spiritual—bringing all of our inherent polarities back into Oneness. Then, becoming One Being with all of creation!

Sacred Union is taking place all around us at this very moment. Learn to see it; learn to feel it within you. Once we align our beings with the everpresent Sacred Union, we will become alive like never before. We will emanate LOVE and Oneness. Our very beingness will serve to dissolve the calcifications of duality, ending the long reign of separation and loneliness.

Sacred Union is the Master Key to everything. It will unlock any door. It will take you to the greatest depths of understanding and lift you to heights of Love presently unimaginable.

THE EIGHTH KEY:

Unifying Our Polarities

Unifying Our Polarities. . .

Sacred Union begins within.

Each of us already contains an internal sacred marriage of male and female. These two polarities have united together into one physical form, our present body. So first, we must become familiar with our own inner male and female. They must be balanced and aligned before we can proceed any further. This is part of the process of the unification of AN, the Sacred Union of our internal Sun & Moon.

To do this, you can begin by covering one side of your face with a sheet of paper. Look into a mirror and carefully study what you see, then reverse the process. Your male polarity will be located on the side of your body which is predominant. So if you are right-handed, your male polarity will be on your right side.

Cover one side of your face and study the polarity which is revealed. Notice what emotions it is showing. You can discover much about yourself by using this practice. Is your polarity happy or sad, tired or a rascal? Get to know it by studying your face in the mirror. You might want to write down a list of what you have discovered. Now reverse the process and study the opposite side of your face. Here is your other polarity. Look closely at the qualities it reveals. Make a list of what you see. Then uncover your entire face and notice how your male and female relate to one another. Again, write down what you see. How do your polarities complement each other? What kind of balance do they have?

It's essential to become familiar with your male and female polarities. Do they need healing or empowerment? If they are not happily merged into Sacred Union and working together as One Being, then you have some work to do. This you can do through visualization or by working with them while studying your face. For example, your male polarity may need more softness or your female more courage. Another practice to heal your polarities is in my book, *The Star-Borne*. As you work on aligning your polarities, you will notice some stunning changes in your life. This will become visible in the map of your face as well.

• Bringing it into your body •

It's important to continually anchor these new levels of awareness into our physical bodies. Remember: there's no more separation between the physical and the spiritual. They're all part of our One Being. So let's stand up and have our male polarity do his mudra to welcome the Sun. *(A mudra is a sacred gesture done with the arms.)* Now have him honor his beloved, the Moon. Incorporate a walk with these mudras. Here's the walk of the Sun and the walk of the Sun honoring the Moon. Continue doing this until it feels graceful and natural.

Then we're going to inhabit our female polarity and have her make her mudra to welcome the Moon. Now, have her honor her beloved, the Sun. Let her walk doing her mudras until she moves naturally. The next step is to unite the walks of the Sun and Moon into one graceful, flowing motion.

Let their individual mudras flow together into one unified movement. Take your reunited Sun & Moon for an extended stroll, feeling how well they merge together. As you do this, you'll feel the separate delineations of male and female blend together and your One Being shall start to take form.

When this happens, you can stop and birth a totally new mudra, the mudra of Sun & Moon united into Oneness or AN. This is a most powerful sacred movement. Each time you do it, it will help bring your polarities into alignment. Practice it often until your inner polarities are fully merged.

• •

Uniting our inner polarities is an important part of creating the foundation of our new True Self.

Our internal Sun and Moon
    must be healed, balanced, and united
        before we can experience full Sacred Union.

Once this occurs, we become embodiments of the energy known as AN—the Sun & Moon merged together into One Being. This is a quantum leap into a heightened level of awareness which extends beyond the paradigm of duality. We can now anchor our beings in the Template of Oneness and become woven into the New Matrix.

THE NINTH KEY:

The
One Heart

The One Heart. . .

The One Heart is the heart of all.

As we move into the Invisible, our old emotional body is immensely transformed. We are in the process of building a totally new emotional body. This is needed to handle the expansive, powerful frequencies of Love in the Spiral of Oneness. If we tried to experience the Greater Love with our old emotional bodies, we would be fried to a crisp. Our old heart chakras are simply not strong enough to transmit such accelerated frequencies of Love. Some of us have tried this and felt it affect our physical hearts, giving us irregular heartbeats, shortness of breath, wild palpitations, etc. It's far better to concentrate on creating your new emotional body before you start evoking the Greater Love.

We all share the same heart.

The One Heart means just that. This heart that we share is far vaster and stronger than our own individual small hearts of our old emotional bodies. To visualize the One Heart, see yourself as part of a circle of people. Look at the space in the center of your sacred circle and see that it is your One Heart. This means that you all share the same heart. Our One Heart is capable of immense Love. It is the heart which cannot be broken, for it operates at a very different vibratory frequency than our old individual heart chakras. It sets the harmonic resonance for the entrance of the Greater Love.

The One Heart is more intimate and open than anything we have previously experienced. It is always open, wide open. When we align ourselves with the One Heart, we open our beings to become transmitters/receivers of the Greater Love. As this increasingly activates, we actually become embodiments of the Greater Love. With our new capacity for Love and our heightened vulnerability and openness, our Love becomes stronger than ever before. There's a great strength in open vulnerability which we can now tap. We no longer have any barriers around our hearts. This means that we feel more than we ever did. And yet there is a detachment from the old emotional distortions which helps us keep our balance even in the greatest emotional storms and dramas.

Loving from the One Heart enables us to love with our full beings, without holding back, without qualifying our love. We can now give and receive Love wholeheartedly, free of previous insecurities, free of the drama of 3D love. It is easy to Love and be Loved deeply, vastly, openly. All the old limits and distortions of Love have effortlessly dissolved. Our new foundation is All-Encompassing Love. This is simply the One Heart loving itself. From here we shall soon experience Ecstatic Love which is the Love experienced by embodying the Lovers from Beyond the Stars.

As our old individual hearts are surrendered and merged into the One Heart, the Greater Love is felt. This greatly surpasses and transcends all previous experiences of love within the Template of Duality. It is a vaster, deeper, wider, All-Encompassing, Truer Love than we have ever known.

This Love is both grounded and full of sublime ecstasy. It is a Love without boundaries which unites us all together in conscious Oneness, establishing the foundation for us to become One Being.

The introduction of the heightened frequencies of Love within the One Heart also present us with some of our greatest challenges. What do we do with our existing relationships which are anchored in duality? How do we release our old relationship roles, responses and attitudes? How do we create the space in our beings and in our lives to experience this Greater Love on a daily basis? The answer is stunningly simple.

We become embodiments of the One Heart, the new Masters of Love.

By embodying the One Heart and making it our new state of normal, everything around us is transformed.

This is a constant process requiring diligent watchfulness on our part. We must learn to discern whether we are coming from duality or Oneness in each moment. Gently unhooking ourselves from duality whenever necessary. Expanding our One Heart until we can embrace everything and everyone in Oneness. Learn to catch yourself as you fall into unconscious responses which tend to limit and freeze your opinions, such as: *"I hate him." "I don't like this color." "I always do it this way." "No-one could ever love me." "I don't deserve this much love." "You are much too good for me."*

Instead of slamming the door shut on new experiences, attitudes and responses by holding onto outdated opinions, why don't you try to stay open and receptive to the entrance of something totally New? If you don't stretch open your old limited attitudes and responses, you will probably be stifled by supreme boredom as the *same old, same old* continually repeats itself. Allow yourself to repattern and recalibrate into Oneness. You can do this by looking at every situation with new eyes, as if you had just arrived on this planet. Check out each situation to see if it is emanating from duality or Oneness. Look at your response. Is it automatic and unconscious or are you responding from the One Heart?

Once you incorporate this into your life, you will find that your being is expanding. Previous limitations dissolve before your very eyes. Suddenly, you feel freer than ever before. A new sense of lightness is introduced into all aspects of your life. And the levels of Love you experience are exponentially increased. Do you know what this is? This is the long awaited and much talked about Ascension.

Ascension is simply the shift in consciousness from duality to Oneness.

Sorry, but it doesn't have anything to do with spaceships coming to take you away, or getting more channeling from the Ascended Masters. Ascension is something that happens within us, not outside. It is our conscious setting ourselves free from the hooks of duality—our rising into Oneness.

THE TENTH KEY:

Earth & Star

Earth & Star. . .

We are the Sacred Marriage of Earth & Star.

Naturally wedded within us are both the physical and spiritual realms of being. By anchoring the Invisible within the physical, we become whole beings. Merging our vastness into our physical bodies quickens us into our full potential as enlivened beings. There is no more separation between the *physical* and the *spiritual*. We are no longer Earth Beings or Starry Beings, but true Earth-Star Beings.

To do this, we must first access our primordial core—our physical, instinctual, Earthly Selves. This is the wild and unbridled, natural part of us which embedded itself in the heart of matter. We need to know our Earthly Selves intimately and to accept this important earthy part of ourselves. Each of us is a microcosm of the Earth. Our DNA contains the seeds and roots of all biology. Our bodies are composed of organic matter—our breath is the wind—our skin the leaves—our eyes the Sun and Moon. Feel yourself as a planet. Your heart is the heartbeat of all creation.

Now see yourself as the starry vastness. Anchor your being there. Feel yourself filled with Light, melting away the confines of your physical form. You are the open-ended universe, stretching beyond infinity. Become the One, embracing everything in your One Heart. Your body has become the map of the entire cosmos containing myriad worlds within worlds.

These two points of Earth & Star represent the furthest extremities of our being. They are the delineations of our known universe. It is important for us to be familiar with them, to be able to access them at all times. The next challenge is to simultaneously anchor our beings at these two extremities of Earth & Star. Center yourself in both the core of physical matter and at the furthest expanse *beyond* the stars.

Sometimes it is helpful to do this with arm movements. Extend one arm high up above your head; your fingertips will represent your Starry pole. Now bring your other arm downwards, fingertips pointing to the ground. This is your Earthly pole.

Stay focused on the Earth-Star poles of your being, while slowly becoming aware of the Spaces-In-Between. Once we make this conscious alignment, we reach yet another level of Sacred Union. Now, simultaneously holding your consciousness in the two extremities of Earth & Star, you will feel a gradual quickening in the Spaces-In-Between.

Earth calls to Star to liberate it;
Star calls to Earth to give it form.

The yearnings of Earth & Star intensify and deepen, sending rolling waves of Love all across the Spaces-In-Between. *(Use your body as a map and feel this process taking place within you.)* As their energies begin to merge, the Star is anchored into the core of the Earth, flooding the planet with Light, loosening the calcification of matter through heightened frequencies of Love.

This heightened Love expands outwards, impermeating everything between the two points into an enhanced state of Sacred Union. With the merger of formless with form, the Invisible becomes visible. *We are the container, the contained and the limitless space around the container.* Once this is achieved, a new, vaster One Being is born.

Making the mundane sacred:

Merging Earth & Star within ourselves brings an end to the artificial separation between the *physical* and the *spiritual*. *Everything is sacred.* Even the most mundane, tiny detail of everyday life is sacred. It's like the old saying, "Yes, we're building the Taj Mahal, so please pass me another brick." Our loftiest ideals are achieved through small moments; minute, steady actions which engage our full being. This is why it is so important to always put our finest efforts into everything we do—to always keep our hearts wide open—and to live life to the fullest, without compromise or self-imposed limitations.

Earth & Star, *physical & spiritual*, are not two opposing forces. They are beloved marriage partners, *balanced, equal complements,* who bring to each other the perfect gifts needed to encompass a new level of wholeness. Once this Sacred Union takes place within you, there will be a tremendous change in your physical body. The vibratory frequencies will quicken, your physical energy will greatly increase, and you will be filled with unbridled joy! You will be both grounded and free. This is how the Invisible is anchored into the Earth and how the Earth is liberated from duality.

THE ELEVENTH KEY:

One Being

One Being...

We are all part of a much Vaster Being.

To activate our One Being, we must let go of our attachment to ourselves as individualized units of consciousness and look larger. We must surrender our primary identification with ourselves as separate beings and see ourselves as part of a much greater whole. When we do this, we realize that we are all part of One Vaster Being. My old analogy of us as points on one vast star of Oneness is useful here. The Star is the map of our One Being.

Once we become One Being, we will discover that we have finally transcended much of our pesky ego selves, the noisy little part of ourselves which was so susceptible to duality. Many still fear this process, afraid that by rising into greater levels of Oneness they will lose themselves. However, by becoming One Being you don't cease to be an individual. We still retain our special uniqueness which are our gifts to the One. We actually become more in alignment with our True Core Selves.

This expansion into One Being is like blowing up a balloon. We move into a vaster level of our True Selves. It feels wonderful and extremely natural, comforting and tremendously liberating, like shedding a weighty, crusty old skin. We feel more Vibrantly Alive than ever before. And there is an unprecedented expansion of Love. We have been stretched beyond all previous boundaries and limitations.

There is never more than One.

Each time we make the expansion into One Being, we access more of our inherent vastness. We are able to enter previously unavailable realms of the invisible. Our One Being creates the receptacle for the heightened energies to enter. It becomes both the womb and the birth canal for the emergence of our New Selves, the ones already woven into the New Matrix. At the same time, we are also extending our base, creating a new foundation from which we can Live Larger.

It's possible to become One Being with any number of beings. We can begin with one other person or with a large group. We can become One Being with animals, rocks, mountains, trees or the planet itself. Once we have become One Being with something or someone, we can never return to our old sense of limited separation with them. Our essences have merged; our One Heart has activated. Together as One, we have stepped beyond our previous boundaries. The membranes to our individual soul envelopes have dissolved to reveal an infinitely vaster Oneness.

Our One Being loves with the One Heart.

When we rise into One Being, we are able to experience stronger, purer Love than ever before through our activated One Heart. We become One Unified Being loving through One Unified Heart. Our One Being's emotional body is far greater than all our old separate heart chakras combined. This greatly expands and magnifies our ability to Love and BE THE LOVE.

Once we are One Being, our responses and attitudes are dramatically transformed. The bonds between the components which comprise our One Being are deep and true. These bonds are founded upon Love, Trust, Openness & Respect. There is a natural and comforting sense of mutual support, deep Love and effortless intimacy. Our Core Selves have joined together in ecstatic Sacred Union. We are here to serve each other with the fullness of our beings. We are ready to give everything and simultaneously, to receive everything.

Many have experienced this expansion into One Being at our Reunions and Master•Classes. This is how we access new levels of energy not experienced before and how we are able to continuously birth the New. Guardians become One Being before taking their positions and hold that enhanced energy for the entire group.

I have been doing this for years; it's how I am able to access highly calibrated levels of consciousness. Whenever I give a talk in a room full of strangers, the first thing I do is scan the audience for ones with whom I can easily align as One Being. There are always some present; check out the far corners of the room and the people directly in front of you. Immediately, I become vaster and my foundation expands. Then, of course, the next step is to activate the One Heart and bring everyone together in Oneness.

We are given continual opportunities to activate our One Being. I have done this on airplanes, in parent-teacher meetings at my children's schools, at boring business meetings, in courtrooms, waiting in lines, at restaurants—wherever people are gathered together. You can do it in an instant and you don't even need to be introduced. It makes life in this unreal world much more fun and you might be amazed at the results. Just watch and see the new spirit of cooperation which develops as everyone's hearts open and your One Being comes alive.

THE TWELFTH KEY:

Neutral Zones

Neutral Zones. . .

Neutral Zones
are stepping stones into the Invisible.

They are islands of neutralized energy interspersed into the planetary energy matrix. Neutral Zones are places of safety and comfort, devoid of their own distinct personality. In a sense, all Neutral Zones feel alike. The energy is swept clean of any outer disturbance, with no psychic residue. There is an evenness and balance which is found nowhere else—an overriding sense of neutrality pervades. Neutral Zones are found all over the planet in small pockets of energy. They should be sought out and utilized by us whenever possible.

In a Neutral Zone you can anchor the Invisible.

Neutral Zones are clear of ancient energies, psychic cacophony and the patternings of duality. They are like a clean slate waiting to be filled. In this atmosphere you can easily access the Invisible as there is nothing to hinder its entrance. Since Neutral Zones are the foundation for our future endeavors, it is important to recognize them. This can best be achieved by scanning the energy and feeling whether it is empty or full of old energies.

Neutral Zones can be found in a variety of locations. They can be located out in nature, or in a hotel room. This is why I often try to stay in modern, business-person type hotels or places with a clean, almost sparse simplicity when I travel. Here, I am most likely to find a Neutral Zone. They won't usually be found in places with a lot of antiques or clutter. You need places which are quiet and clean with undisturbed fresh energies.

Since I travel often and stay in innumerable hotel rooms, I have developed a great respect for the work done by hotel maids. I find that they are doing us a remarkable service. It's fascinating to watch as they enter a room with lots of unsettled, personal energy and quietly neutralize it. Hotel maids are masters of neutralization. It's an important skill, so I try to learn from them. They wipe everything clean, cleaning not only the room, but somehow managing to smooth out the energy at the same time. When they are finished, the room is like new again, an empty receptacle waiting to be filled.

If possible, you should turn at least one room, if not your whole home, into a Neutral Zone. This will become an oasis for you. It will be easy to anchor Oneness here and to maintain your clarity. Begin by clearing out the clutter. Cluttered objects reflect a cluttered mind. Clean out the old. Wipe everything clean and smooth. This doesn't mean that you have to strip away your favorite possessions. Just make everything which remains meaningful or something which creates beauty and inner peace. To maintain your Neutral Zone, you must smooth out and renew the energy each day.

Neutral Zones out in nature are rarely found in the big power places and major vortexes. Too many energies are focused there to allow for the quiet, clear simplicity needed in a Neutral Zone. You also won't find them in areas that still hold a residue of trauma. This includes forests which have been brutally cut down and have since regrown or places where battles once took place. Look instead for those hidden pockets of clear energy which are all around us. These aren't usually the flashy places of stunning beauty, but have a certain, special quality of calm serenity.

Get to know the Neutral Zones in your area. And as you travel, try as much as possible to go from Neutral Zone to Neutral Zone. This will greatly aid you in Living Large on a small planet.

Wizened Innocence

As you step deeper into the Invisible, your own being will become a Neutral Zone. This will occur as you let go of your personal preferences and enter a state of what we call wizened innocence. This wizened innocence is obtained after you have completed the journey from child-like innocence through experience and wisdom to arrive at a new level of wonder. This is a wonder based on the letting go of your previous knowledge and experience. When you, yourself, are a Neutral Zone, you will emanate a vibration of serenity and Love. This will help to smooth out the energy wherever you are.

THE THIRTEENTH KEY:

Null Zones

Null Zones. . .

Null Zones create the womb of the New.

A Null Zone is established after there has been an expansion or flowering outwards of energy which receives some sort of blow or shock, causing it to collapse inwards upon itself. The old, established energy patterns have now been broken. There is no way that they will ever return to their previous patterning. They have been irrevocably changed. The energy of a Null Zone feels jagged and raw. There is much hurt and pain. It's the shattering of a world or a belief system, a long held desire, or sometimes, an important relationship. This shattering creates the perfect foundation for the introduction of something entirely new. The potential for rebirth from the ashes of a Null Zone is enormous.

Null Zones can occur within a defined geophysical area, such as a country, city or region. Wars always create them, as do political upheavals, economic distress, famine and disease. Some of the current geographical Null Zones on the planet are in the former Yugoslavia, ex-Soviet Union, ex-Eastern Germany, as well as Rwanda, Burundi, Somalia and Algeria. Countries such as Cambodia, Lebanon, Tibet, Afghanistan, Haiti, Northern Ireland, China and Ethiopia are still trying to recover from recent experiences of Null Zoning. Vietnam, the Czech Republic, Peru and Chile are good examples of countries which have Null Zoned and are now beginning to renew themselves. Potential future Null Zone areas include: the United States, Mexico, Egypt, Israel, France and India.

Geophysical Null Zones become like black holes, magnetically drawing energy into themselves. They amplify and destabilize whatever inherent discord is present in the surrounding areas. Therefore, it's of utmost importance that the One Heart is anchored on the edges of these Null Zone frontiers. This is why I have made several trips in recent years to Finland, Germany, Slovenia and Croatia. There are now strong, activated groups of magnificent, dedicated people who are anchoring the One Heart in the first three of these countries. This powerful anchoring of Oneness stops the further spread of Null Zones in those regions of the world.

There are also Null Zones created by natural phenomena such as earthquakes, hurricanes, floods, volcanoes and other so called *Acts of God*. Although devastating on the physical plane, often they do not bring the lasting pain and deep shattering of energies as do Null Zones caused by mankind. The old patterns may be temporarily halted, but they are not always irrevocably smashed to bits. Usually, the people who have been affected by natural disasters doggedly rebuild what was damaged, adhering as much as possible to the previous patterning. However these types of Null Zones are extremely useful opportunities to accelerate our growth by transforming our inner attitudes, shifting our value systems, and altering our outer habits and patterns. To experience a natural disaster is a grand opportunity to master the Art of Surrendering and breakthrough into something New.

Sometimes, the death of a leader will cause a Null Zone. For example, the assassination of President Kennedy in the United States in 1963. This didn't Null Zone the country, but it Null Zoned our innocence and idealism. Or a death or scandal involving the head of an organization can Null Zone that entire group. Families can Null Zone when something shatters their unity. Remember, a Null Zone is not just a temporary crisis, it is a permanent breaking of established energy patterns.

Most, if not all, large cities have areas within them which are Null Zones. These inner city Null Zones are like painful, open wounds which affect the entire surrounding area. If only this was realized by the inhabitants of the whole city, then perhaps, they would see the importance of healing the pain in their midst. If there's a hungry homeless person out in the cold, they are the reflection of that part of us which feels abandoned. We're all part of the Vaster Being. And if any part of our Vaster Being is suffering, we all feel it. It's the same when we have a toothache. It's not just the tooth's problem; it's something which affects our entire body. We can't expect the tooth to take itself to the dentist to be fixed; instead we must unite together and use our entire body to manifest the needed healing.

Null Zones can also occur within our own beings.

What causes us to Null Zone? It's much the same as with the outer world: the shattering of a long held ideal, the dissolving of an important relationship, a sudden cataclysmic shock to our prevailing belief system, the misuse of drugs, the loss of our job, a serious illness; mental, emotional or physical trauma, etc. When any of these things happen, your world begins collapsing around you and within you.

There's another type of Null Zone which can occur when you have greatly expanded your being into the Invisible. This is caused by a sudden, unexpected infusion of duality when you are in a most delicate state of being so dissolved and expanded that you barely exist. This is the most extremely painful type of Null Zoning. It feels like all the worlds within worlds are collapsing upon you, within you. Like a gigantic house of cards, *falling, falling.* As yet, I haven't learned how to avert this once it begins, although I've certainly tried.

After you have Null Zoned, what happens? Your world has collapsed and you are in a lot of pain. You sit amidst the sharp, shattered shards of what you once knew and believed in. Everything is either broken or gone. Allow yourself to cry and mourn the loss of the old. This is part of the grieving process and actually accelerates the full Null Zone experience. At this point, don't even consider trying to put things back to where they used to be. It's not only unwise, but it's absolutely impossible. Imagine trying to reglue an exquisitely intricate sculpture created out of impossibly thin strands of handblown glass. Even if you managed to put some pieces together, it would not be a pretty sight. And it would certainly not be the same sculpture you had before.

Accept your Null Zone.

Accept that the past is gone, now part of the *Past That Never Was.* Your probable future is gone as well, part of the *Future Which Never Shall Be.* And please remember that Null Zones happen for a purpose. They actually occur to help us break free from old, stagnant patterns, giving us an unique opportunity for a quantum leap into a deeper sector of the Unknown. Null Zones are the womb of the New.

Phoenixes are reborn from the ashes.

They are reborn from the ashes, not flower beds or idyllic situations. Well, look about you! See all the ashes from yesterday's belief system. You're now in a perfect position to be reborn. And don't be in a hurry to recreate your reality. That's like trying to glue the glass sculpture back into its old form. Be empty for awhile. Be devastated. Be bereft of belief systems. Revel in your openness and freedom from the past. Don't hold onto anything. Now this may be quite uncomfortable; it often is. But so what! You've been stretched beyond your comfort zone and that's never easy or comfortable. Accept this as graciously as possible.

Now take a good look around you and check out your options. That's right, you don't have any! There's no place to go except to somewhere you've never been before—the totally New. Congratulations, you're doing really well. Perhaps, since you're in the womb of the New, this is the perfect time to birth your True Self.

THE FOURTEENTH KEY:

I-Await

I-Await. . .

I-Await is a state of heightened receptivity found within the womb of the Invisible.

This heightened receptivity or active passivity is utilized while we are waiting in the womb of the Invisible for the New to manifest. There is a vast difference between ordinary waiting and the state of I-Await. And there is certainly no sense of boredom involved. I-Await is an elegant emptiness. It is neither the sitting back passively and lamely hoping for things to happen, nor is it going out forcefully to make them happen. Rather, it is an active aliveness, combined with a total willingness to give your all. From this place of heightened openness, we surrender everything and immerse ourselves into the waves of the Invisible.

Here we become like leaves on the water, floating on the Invisible currents which lead us to our next step. We feel this huge wave of the Invisible all around us, flowing right through us. An air of rising expectancy imbues each moment. We can feel that we are being deeply transformed, and yet it seems to take such a long time for these changes to appear on the physical. We long to align our transformed inner beings with a new physical reality, for we have discovered that our New Selves no longer fit into the limited patterning of our old lives.

Now we need to let go of our sense of urgency and accept that everything is happening within its perfect timing. Surrender again to the waves. Float like a leaf. . . In I-Await we remain alert and vibrantly alive. Our old worlds have shattered and we have completed our long process of dying. We are floating in the womb, awaiting the birth of our New Selves and new world.

*Every act of completion
contains within it
the seeds of the New.*

While we are awaiting the New, we can occupy ourselves with the myriad details of completion. But we soon discover that the act of completion itself has greatly transformed. Previously, when we completed things in the Template of Duality, we had to complete in order to experience the new beginning at a later time. Now we find that completion and new beginnings are indelibly woven together in Oneness. Each act of completion we do has seeded in it our new beginnings. There is no more separation. It has become one unified process of completion / beginning. This makes the act of completion easier and far more enjoyable.

THE FIFTEENTH KEY:

Unpinning from Time

Unpinning From Time. . .

Time and Space are illusory measurements of duality.

The time/space continuum has served as the definitive boundaries of our duality-based reality system. It is the framework for all our Earthly endeavors. This illusory, duality-imposed measurement helps keep us imprisoned within the old spiral. It delineates our activities within the old map. We build our lives around these false units of measurement without question. Habit patterns are developed to help strengthen their sense of reality. But are time and space real?

Earthly time is simply an abstract, illusory energy which can be stretched and stopped at will, using only our purest intentions. This liberation from the limitations of time gives us endless opportunities for Living Larger than ever before. There are numerous practical applications for this in our daily lives. But first, you must learn to stop time. The practice for this is given in my book, *11:11–Inside the Doorway.* When time stops, you enter the zone of No-Time.

"Time is an imposition on the Greater Reality, but it also serves a Purpose. To recreate the Greater Reality while living in the midst of the illusion of time is our challenge.

Time and space can be perceived as a fine mesh which has been created to sift and filter formless Essence. This sifting of formless Essence through the mesh of time and space separates the elements which are predestined to be joined together.

When formless Essence passes through the mesh of time and space, experiencing the illusion of separation, a heightened yearning to return to Oneness is created. This yearning causes a quickening within the individual units of consciousness which leads to profound transformation." . . . *from the Temple Invisible.*

No-Time is the measurement of the Greater Reality.

As we become Masters of Time, we learn how to live in an enduring state of No-Time. To live each moment of every day in this enhanced measurement of time in the pool of endless potential.

• Unpinning Ourselves from Time •

One of our prerequisites for Living Large is to unpin ourselves from the confines of time and space. So take off your watches and get ready to experience a deeper level of freedom. Let's begin by taking a closer look at time. We have these twenty-four hour periods divided into what are labeled days and nights. Generally, days are defined as when the sky is light, nights are when it is dark. On a more esoteric level they can be seen as periods of rulership of the Sun and Moon.

Since birth we have been programmed to align our activities with the cycles of days and nights. In the morning we are supposed to get up and have a meal called breakfast. Then we work until midday when we eat another meal. This is usually followed by another period of activity, although some cultures have a rest phase following the noon meal. In the evening we eat once again, then partake in recreational activities until we go to sleep for the rest of the night. That's pretty much the normal schedule. By aligning our beings to this rigid schedule, we stay pinned into the time/space continuum.

Various assumptions, habits and belief systems have been built up around this continuum.
Some examples are:

• *We need a certain amount of sleep in order to function.*

• *We need to eat regularly in order to stay healthy.*

• *In the daytime we are awake; at night we are asleep.*

• *There is never enough time to do everything.*

We are actually much Larger beings than we realize and are inherently free from the confines of time and space. We have always been anchored into the Greater Reality and just have to remove some of the coverings to be there in our full consciousness. When we unpin ourselves from time and space, we can free ourselves from our old limiting habits.

First, we must look at everything with new eyes, as if we had just arrived on this planet. Remove the pins which have held you in the clutches of time and space. Pretend for a minute that you are on a planet whose days and nights last only for a few hours, making it impossible to schedule your usual activities into the old slots. Since we no longer have a tidy schedule to follow, we must instead be led by our own natural inclinations, learning to eat when we are hungry, sleep when we are tired, create when we are inspired.

Once we are unpinned, everything accelerates and the energies are heightened. The vibrations have quickened immeasurably. We have moved into the eternal No-Time of the Greater Reality. Now, let's take a new look at some of our old assumptions:

• **We need a certain amount of sleep each night in order to function.**

We can function quite well on no sleep if necessary. When you are in a heightened state of unpinning, you can carry on for days with little or no sleep and not even be tired. *(My personal record for this is eight days without sleep. A few nights during this phase I slept for an hour or two. Throughout, I functioned fine, although I was definitely in an altered consciousness.)* Sometimes, you will require lots of sleep, especially in times of deep processing and recalibration of energies. That's fine; always honor your needs.

• **In the daytime we are awake; at night we are asleep.**

Please don't feel that once you are in bed for the night, you must stay there until morning. If you awaken in the middle of the night, it's often for a good reason. Whenever you awaken, feel the energies; what's happening around you? You might want to step outside for a few moments and look at the natural world. Often we are awakened to see something truly mystical in the heavens. Maybe it's time to get up and do something creative. The middle of the night is very special. The world is quiet and the normal psychic cacophony has lessened. It's a perfect time for writing, contemplation or exploring the Invisible. Learn to open up your nights and liberate your being.

Our entire approach to sleep is in the process of immense transformation. One of the main functions of sleep was to give us time to access our unconscious. As we increasingly merge our unconscious with our conscious being and express our True Self, we will find that we need little sleep. This requires that we take time each day to practice the art of not-doing—being still and letting go of the world around us, while melting into Oneness.

Another way that we can replenish our beings is to step into heightened No-Time. I often do this when I'm tired and have absolutely no time to rest. Lie down for a few minutes and totally dissolve your being into Oneness. Don't go to sleep; simply let your molecules melt into the Matrix of Oneness until you no longer have a physical form. Everything becomes very abstract and floating.

There will be a deep release of the tension caused by keeping yourself in physical form. As you do this, a small part of you will remain alert enough to hear the sounds in the room, while the rest of you no longer exists as an individual being. You can float for what seems to be aeons, then look at your watch and find that only five minutes have passed. When you arise, you will be totally refreshed!

• *We need to eat regularly in order to stay healthy.*

When the Surf is up and you become unpinned from time and space, you really don't need physical food. Your nourishment comes from the accelerated energies around you.

You are fed with Light frequencies and Love. This is a similar experience to losing your appetite when you first fall in love. It is quite different from fasting which is a spiritual discipline or starving which is being deprived of food while you are in a normal state of consciousness.

When you do become hungry, you should eat. But please don't feel that you need to eat certain foods because of the time of day. *You can eat whatever you want, whenever you want.* Throw away the concept of breakfast, lunch & dinner. Let go of the idea of three meals a day. Eat with an open mind and a hungry stomach.

There are certain times when we want to eat copious amounts of food. This often occurs when we're undergoing emotional trauma or feeling a lack of love and companionship in our life. These cases can best be dealt with by adjusting and expanding our attitudes towards Love, learning to see that Love constantly surrounds us. As we become embodiments of the Greater Love, these food cravings will cease.

An intense desire for food can also signify a period of significant adjustment, such as happens after we have greatly expanded our beings and now try to integrate these changes into our everyday lives. In this case, I usually eat and eat. These cravings cease when the energies have been integrated. Sometimes when you need extra grounding, you will eat more than usual. Just make sure that this isn't your only form of grounding and that your enhanced eating is only temporary, and you will be fine.

Our entire approach to food is in the midst of immense transformation. Something very new is coming. I don't yet know how this will manifest. It could be the introduction of new foods, new ways of combining foods, or perhaps, we will transcend eating altogether. In the meanwhile, during this somewhat confusing time of transition, it is best to follow the promptings of your body which will tell you what is most appropriate to eat. For some this is a healthy regimen of whole foods, others may need to eat the denser foods in order to remain grounded. Whatever you choose to eat, do it consciously, with awareness and gratitude. And always remain open to the introduction of the New.

• ***There is never enough time to do everything.***

By Mastering Time we can stretch it out to allow us all the time in the world. We can also speed it up when needed. We can treat time like the fluid energy it really is, utilizing this energy whenever needed.

THE SIXTEENTH KEY:

Unpinning from Space

Unpinning from Space...

Space is the measurement of the distance between separate objects on the physical plane.

It is defined by a sense of *here and there.* In order to have a viable concept of space, you must first believe in the illusion of separation. Once you anchor your being in Oneness, that sense of separation dissolves. Space enlarges and becomes all-encompassing. There is no more distance between things. No more *here and there.* Everything is embraced in Oneness. Standing in any given point within the One, we have direct, immediate access to all. It's similar to a hologram. If you can see any part of the hologram, you can access all of it.

Once you understand this, you will discover that by anchoring yourself in your vastness through Living Large, you can transcend the limitations of distance. If we narrow ourselves down to only the physical 3D perspective, distance will persist. But since we are far more than mere physical beings, it's quite easy to unpin ourselves from space.

Being unpinned has numerous practical applications in our everyday lives. We can utilize this in our friendships with people who live far away. We feel them right next to us at all times. You can have some great interactions, and don't even need to write letters! If you want to know how a certain part of the world is feeling, simply tune in. It's right here, interwoven with you in the matrix of Oneness.

• Travel Tips for the Unpinned •

Being unpinned from the concepts of time and space is quite useful while traveling. I travel all over the world and use these techniques wherever I go. They really work and make traveling much easier and infinitely more enjoyable. *Here are a few examples:*

• Airplanes •

First, become as large as the airplane, then merge with it and become One Being. This greatly enhances your air safety, since the physical airplane has now been woven into the heightened energies of Oneness. Now embrace all of your fellow passengers and the flight crew in the One Heart. Watch out for this one; sometimes it has very powerful effects. I've been on some flights so filled with Love that I didn't want to get off the plane. You'll discover that this process heightens the efficiency of the flight attendants as well. Meals really get served fast!

Now sit back and relax, placing yourself in the state of No-Time. You will feel a clear channel of light open up between your point of departure and your destination. Your airplane will glide through this channel, effortlessly taking you to where you want to go. You will not notice the passing of the hours, for you will be resting in that timeless instant of No-Time. I am one who cannot sleep on airplanes because there's too much psychic energy crammed into a small space, and this really helps me stay in a clear place.

While we're on the subject of airplanes, here's a little practice I discovered for calming down turbulence. I don't know why, but it seems to work. When the airplane gets bumpy, put your feet on the floor with your legs uncrossed. Place your hands, palms down on your thighs. Now raise your hands 4-8 inches off your legs. Put lots of energy into your arms and hands until they become somewhat rigid. They now become stabilizers for the airplane. Keep strong energy flowing into your forearms and hands until the airplane is once again calm. Many of us have tried this procedure and for some reason, it works!

• Cars •

When traveling by car, it's important to align yourself to the frequency band of energy which goes from your departure point to your destination. Do this before you even start the motor. Feel the waves of the Invisible which lead to your proposed destination and hop on them. Then start your car. Driving on the subtle currents of the Invisible is a new experience. It's almost like driving with an autopilot. You can sit back and enjoy the ride.

Driving on the subtle energy waves is most helpful when you are utterly lost. When this happens, the best course of action is to forego thinking and strongly tune into the waves. Follow them unquestionably as they lead you to turn this way and that, and eventually, they will take you right to the doorstep of where you wanted to go.

But I should probably warn you that once in a while, something unexpected may happen. Sometimes, your car or the waves might decide that it would rather go somewhere other than your proposed destination. If this happens, you can either follow the energy and see where it leads you or be alert enough to catch this deviation from your chosen route and take charge of your vehicle. This may sound strange, but it has happened to the best of us. I've personally had lots of unexpected adventures when the waves pulled me in a different direction than the one I thought I was on. I've visited the Santa Fe flea market—*(great shopping)*, seen films when I thought I was on my way home—*(enjoyed them all)*, and been led on numerous wild adventures.

Once in Patzcuaro, Mexico the energies pulled me away from my appointed destination and took me to the shores of a lake, out of my car, onto a boat to an island in the center of the lake, up the hill to the top of the island where there was a monolithic statue of a man with his clenched fist upraised to the sky. Immediately, a little Indian girl approached and took me by the hand, leading me around the base of the statue. She sang to me all the while, a charming song in an ancient language. Completing our journey around the statue, she bowed and disappeared without a word. Then the energies pulled me down the hill, past all the shops which I would have liked to visit, past all the restaurants with their delicious smelling food, onto a boat which was just pulling away from the dock, back across the lake, and redeposited me in my car where I sat in stunned silence for some time, having totally forgotten my original destination.

Another thing which might happen while driving your car is distance leaping. This means that you might cover a distance which takes seven hours to travel in half that time. This isn't achieved by breaking the speed records, but by being unpinned. It certainly makes car travel easier. Of course, you must stay extra alert or you may go zooming past your destination, assuming it's not due for several more hours. Also, if there are any places you wish to visit enroute, you better program them in before you set off on your journey. Otherwise, they might be in the segment which you have leapt over; in which case, you won't even see any sign of them. It will be as if they had never existed. Traveling by car while unpinned is a constant adventure.

• Boats •

Boats are a special case, for all boats large and small, can lead you deeper into the Invisible. There's something about the fact that you are in the water which acts as a catalyst to propel you further into the Invisible. The next time you are on a boat, see yourself on the Celestial Barge, traveling into the deep Unknown. Then feel what happens! By being aware of where you really are, you will have fascinating experiences and profound revelations while traveling by boat.

Kilo O Kalani Nui I Mamao.

Traveling by boat often triggers deep memories within us. This is especially true of sailing ships and canoes. Many of our ancient migrations upon this planet have been made by sea. The indigenous people of the Pacific Ocean have much experience in this form of travel. This is especially true of the Polynesian and Micronesian people, some of whom still hold an advanced knowledge of celestial navigation upon the subtle currents. They are Masters of the Waves and know how to align themselves to prevailing currents and the position of certain star systems. Some of them still carry stories of our first migration to this planet through the starwaves from *Beyond the Beyond*. And I've heard that in those most ancient of times, the sailors would get in their canoes with great readiness, and instead of traveling forth, they would sing their destinations to them. This sounds a lot like I-Await.

THE SEVENTEENTH KEY:

Relating to Relationships

Relating to Relationships. . .

Relationships:
Our ultimate challenge & final frontier.

Relationships have always been one of our key issues and supreme challenges. We desperately yearn for them, and then once we are in them, often feel stifled and disappointed. This is because most relationships are still bound in the confines of duality. This has distorted and affected almost all aspects of relationships. Sadly, our dysfunctional relationship model has become the accepted norm.

The new levels of relationship are in the process of being created. Once again, we're the midwives in this birth. And of course, we're also the guinea pigs, the ones who get to experiment until we discover exactly what these new forms of relationship are. Life in the laboratory of Love is not going to be dull, and it's definitely going to challenge us to Live Large. *Here's a few helpful hints to get us started:*

• How cleanly do we relate? •

Relationships are a sharing of essence and a transfer of energies between two or more people. It's also a merger of auric fields. Thus, it's vitally important that we make our interactions with one another as clean and pure as possible. We need to be open, honest and respectful with each other at all times.

There are many murky habits we have acquired which hold us back from relating cleanly. Most of these are unconsciously embedded within us and it's important to find them and root them out right now. Please check and see if you are doing any of these habits. Here are some of the ways that we misuse energy:

the Energy Takers:

Ones who come up to you and start pulling at your energy, trying to get it for themselves. Perhaps, these are shamans-in-training, practicing the petty stealing of power when there's an inexhaustible supply available. They'll say, "Oh, I just love your energy!" as they try to grab it away. Still locked into horizontal energy, they would rather feed off secondhand energy than tap into the universal supply.

the Glommers:

Glommers are a bit more extreme than normal energy takers. They are exceedingly invasive in their approach. They will come up to you and attach themselves to you like parasites. It's a horrible sensation and reminds me of those sea creatures with suction cups on their feet. Perhaps, all they seek is union, but their method is certainly distorted. When you've been glommed on, you will feel a heavy, thick weight attaching onto you. It's *not* a pleasant sensation. I try to avoid glommers whenever possible. But if I do get glommed, I remove them from me immediately. It's a deep invasion of energy and you should watch that you don't do it to anyone. Glommers are usually totally unconscious of what they are doing.

the Sludge:

These are people who are constantly discharging their stagnant energy all around them. This discarded energy is like a thick sludge which sticks to everything. It's a disgusting, almost sickening energy, similar to a swamp full of rotting matter. Often sludge is discharged by sighing, coughing, crying, belching, and farting. If you are a carrier of sludge, then you need to find other methods to clear the toxins from your system. Do some form of purification such as fasting, colonics, a shifting of diet and combine it with regular exercise. Spend time outdoors. This will get rid of the reservoir of stagnant energy within you. And you will feel remarkably better.

the Pretenders:

Pretenders are those who pretend that they are something which they are not. Strong people who claim to be weak or needy. Smart people who pretend to be dumb. Unsure people who fake confidence; confidant people who pretend to be unsure, etc. Have you ever asked yourself why you are doing this? Perhaps, you think that you will be better liked if you disguise your true capabilities. But better liked by whom? If someone's approval of you depends on being something you're not, then get them out of your life and get real! It's OK to be strong, weak, capable and fragile, as long as that's how you really are. Be honest with yourself *before* you relate to others. Otherwise, all your relationships will be built on false foundations and you will always be repressed.

the Tamperers:

Tamperers just can't resist trying to alter someone's energy. Using horizontal energy, they sidle up to us and with a little touch here and a subtle touch there, they try to break into the code of our beings. The worst thing is that many tamperers are totally unconscious of what they are doing. They'll often use a series of short taps on the inside of your wrists or your back to try to tamper with your energy. My belief about tamperers is that they are carrying around with them an energy which is not their true essence, perhaps, that of another entity. The cure is to strip yourself down to your Core Self where there is no energy except for your own stripped-down Self. And stay there!

the Possessors:

Possessors want ALL of you, all of the time. They want to know where you are every moment. They are wracked by uncontrollable jealousy and overwhelming fears which are masked in the name of love. How insecure they are. Often angry and demanding, possessors feel that they will lose their relationship if they let go of their control for an instant. Thus, they hold on tighter and tighter until the object of their affections either suffocates, escapes or becomes disempowered.

the Sponge:

Sponges define themselves solely by their relationship role. "I am Mrs. Charles Jabadar." "I am Nina's husband." They have lost their own identity. They eat what their partner eats, listen to the music their partner likes, etc. Whatever, their partner does, they will do. Sponges have become almost an extra appendage of their partner, like a third arm. Well dear ones, one of these days you're going to have to look at the Big Question—Who are you really?

the Limp Rag:

Limp rags love being dependent. In fact, they probably have never tried independence. They sit around in the corners of life and let others do it for them. It's as if they checked out before they ever checked in. Since limp rags don't like to put out any of their own energy, *(talk about energy conservation!)*, they require lots of time, effort and energy from you. Be prepared to make all the decisions, shoulder all the responsibilities and carry your limp rags around with you. If you are a limp rag, it's time to look deeply inside yourself and find the hidden denial. Why are you afraid of living? Perhaps, since you have a physical body, it might be appropriate to finally come to life.

As you can see by this long, but not nearly comprehensive list, it's vitally important to maintain the clarity and integrity of your energy. How can you have a healthy relationship until you are clean and balanced with your energy?

We should also look out for those unconscious, pre-programmed responses which we use when we relate with others. Some of these we have acquired as "social graces", things like shaking hands when we greet each other, and inquiring, "How are you?", when we really don't care how the other person is doing. Or if we are asked that same question, we are always supposed to respond, "I'm doing fine.", because no-one really wants to know if you're not.

Then there's the New Age response of staring intensely at each other's eyes. For hours. . . What this does is lock you into the third eye energies. It certainly does not bring you into a deeper Oneness.

Less is always More.

We are working with subtle energies in the Invisible. *Less is more*. We don't have to make those big, hearty hugs to feel close to someone. A light touch of the fingertips is so much stronger. And cleaner. Again. . . BE REAL. Be Light. Once your energy is clear, it's time to make room for Love!

• Make room in your life for Love •

If your life is cluttered with activities and superficial friendships, if you're always zooming about here and there, if you don't have a second to yourself, how are you going to fit in a relationship? Partnerships are like gardens; they need lots of space in which to grow. They need sunlight, nurturing and attention. Not to mention constant weeding. Do you have time for a relationship?

If not, and if you want one, you should start clearing some space for it right now, *before* it arrives in your life. (The same is true if you want to recalibrate an already existing relationship.) Remember that the New is born out of emptiness, not clutter. It's a pregnant emptiness, which means that you have done the needed work on yourself and are prepared to go wherever the waves may take you.

Once you have created an empty openness around you, sit in the heightened receptivity of I-Await. Until that relationship manifests itself, you can shift your consciousness from being alone to All-One. Be in love with everything!

• Be the Love •

If we want to experience real Love, then first we must embody it. Become a Master of Love. We must be in a constant state of loving. Loving everyone, everything, whom we encounter. LIVE LOVE. Whenever you go out into the world, spread that Love around. Give each person you meet some of that Love. This includes the people working in restaurants, banks, gas stations, wherever you go. Don't forget the strangers passing by on the street. Love them!

And don't limit your Love to people. Love the wild creatures as well; even the flies and spiders. Love the rain, the rocks, the streets, your frying pan, the trees, your furniture. I once read a great story about Carl Jung who was a brilliant being, and how each morning when he walked into his kitchen, he greeted all his cooking pots. He had the right idea and knew that even so-called inanimate objects have a life-force. Everyone and everything here on Earth needs Love.

• Birth your New Self first •

We want to experience the *new* types of relationship, right? You know what this means, don't you? It means that before we can live in the New, we first have to become New Beings. Otherwise, we could be presented with the most glorious partner right here & now and we wouldn't know what to do with them! We'd just bring out our old ways of relating which we learned in duality.

So first, please unhook yourself from duality, transform your emotional body and align it with the One Heart, learn to Live Large and birth your New Self. This exponentially increases our chances of having successful relationships.

Equal Partnerships are the foundation of the New Relationships

Now let's talk about the alignment with your partner in this New Relationship. If you already have one, it's time to take a good look at who you have chosen. If you don't have one, let's look at our criteria for a partner. What type of person are you drawn to? Is this person needy or dependent? Can they survive without you? Or do you need this person to save, shelter, support or protect you? *Oops, look out!* If either of you is not strong, clear, whole and independent, or comes from a place of neediness or lack, then this isn't going to be the kind of New Relationship you want. If you're still playing the role of stalwart savior or helpless victim needing rescue, you should drop it right now.

How supportive are you of each other's goals, values and spiritual aspirations? Is there mutual respect in your relationship? Do you genuinely like each other? These are all important components of a New Relationship.

Two wholes make an even Greater Wholeness.

Equality in partnership is vitally important. We must each be whole beings within ourselves before we begin the process of establishing healthy, real relationships anchored in the One Heart. There must be an overall balance, equality, and symmetry between the partners on the physical, emotional, mental and spiritual levels. You can only share as much of your being as the other person is capable of or willing to receive.

• On the Physical •

Let's check out the different levels of your beings and see how they balance. First, we'll look at the physical. How do your energy levels compare to each other? If one person is bristling with vitality and their partner is always tired, then there is an obvious imbalance. Sometimes this is a sign that one person is draining the other or that someone has a leak in their auric field. You and your partner can have quite different personalities and still get along well, but it helps if you have similar levels of physical vitality and aliveness. It's even better if they appreciate your sense of humour!

When one partner is overweight and the other is very thin: this may signify that someone is taking more than their share from the relationship. Or it may be an indicator of imbalance on the emotional level. One partner is suppressing their emotions while the other is compensating for feeling unloved. They are both in a lot of emotional pain.

There are so many levels which need to be in balance within an equal partnership. There's the matter of responsibility. Make sure that one partner isn't consistently carrying the full load while the other is lying back and enjoying the ride; if they are, you have an obvious imbalance.

How natural do you feel when you are togther? Do you feel comfortable being naked with each other? Do you like your partner's natural scent? Do you feel attractive with them? These are all important considerations.

There's also the matter of your value systems. Are they aligned and similar? Do you both want the same things in life? What's important to each of you? Are they enduring qualities or material objects? If one person want to have a glamorous cosmopolitan lifestyle and the other wants to live simply on a farm, how are they ever going to be happy together? It's important to have an alignment of value systems.

• On the Emotional •

Now look at your emotional bodies. Are you both anchored in the One Heart? If one of you isn't, then the expression of your Love is going to be greatly hindered. It will be like trying to pour the ocean into a small cup. I'm sure you know what it is like to openly give your love to someone who can't accept it or becomes frightened at the vastness of your feelings. There are also those who are frightened at the depth of their own latent emotions and keep them tightly locked up. These are all the imbalances of duality's *small hearts/small love* syndrome. Loving in the One Heart brings an end to all those unbalanced relationships between the *Givers* and the *Takers*. Now we can both give everything and receive everything. What a stunning difference.

• On the Mental •

Being equals on the mental level is very important. This doesn't mean that you have to know the same things or think in identical ways. Often our differences in knowledge or even our various approaches to learning are what give us tremendously stimulating creative sparks. But whatever paths you took to acquire your knowledge, although they might be totally different, should have led you to a similar level of understanding. I know that some people are quite fond of the old mentor-student types of relationship, but these are not equal partnerships. They are often based on issues of control and superiority and usually fall apart when the student finally reaches a level where they realize that they can learn more without their mentor. In fact, getting free of their mentor is the biggest breakthrough they can make.

These superior-inferior relationships are doomed from the start. And they are often quite unfair and painful to the one in the student position who unconsciously yearns for equality, but knows that it can never be reached with their more experienced or advanced partner. This keeps them in a constant state of feeling inferior and disempowered. Yet, if they were in an equal relationship with someone at a similar level of understanding, these feelings of inferiority would quickly disappear.

When one chooses to play the role of superior, there is often a hidden fear of equal partnerships which are perceived of as too challenging and uncomfortable. With your student partner, there's no-one around to question your entrenched habits and belief systems, no-one to push you past your comfort zone. Which is exactly what you most need. So mentor-student relationships are a lose-lose situation, unnatural partnerships which keep you hooked into duality.

• On the Spiritual •

Alignment of Essence within your Core Selves and an equality in levels of spiritual awareness and attainment is extremely important in an equal partnership. Check out your belief systems and see how they match up. If one person is an avid churchgoer and the other one is off exploring the Invisible, how are you going to communicate with one another across the chasm of disparate belief systems? We can always keep our spiritual life separate and private, but haven't we done that before? Isn't it time to openly live our deepest and highest Truths?

This alignment of spiritual belief systems has never been as important as now. If you want to experience an expanded relationship in the New, both of you must first be anchored in the Template of Oneness. These choices to step free of duality must be made individually by each person involved because it is what they are truly called to do, and these choices cannot be faked for the sake of the relationship.

New Relationships don't fit into old patterns.

Another thing which we should be aware of is the outdated relationship patterning which we try to adhere to. Since it is an outgrowth of duality, our present relationship model is doomed to failure no matter how hard we try to make successful partnerships. First, there's all those old roles that we have assumed. The ingrained behavior patterns that are assigned to the roles of husband and wife, man and woman. Many of these need to be thrown away so we can start with a totally clean slate. Then there are the habits of relating we have acquired through our past experiences of duality-based partnerships. They have to be wiped clean, so we can respond in refreshingly new ways.

Also take a good look at your relationship and see if it is based on karmic obligations. The vast majority of existing relationships on Earth today are still trying to fulfill old karmic debts and promises, or seeking revenge for past injustices. And while this might be a viable basis for a partnership in the Template of Duality, it certainly isn't anymore. Not if you want a New Relationship that's actually going to be healthy, balanced and fulfilling. Karma doesn't exist in the Template of Oneness, so anchor your being there and let karma go! It's only an illusion anyway. *You don't owe anyone anything, except perhaps your own Higher Self.* And you are not responsible for anyone's happiness except your own. Be true to your Core Self at all times, emanate Love and truth, and follow your heart. Be real. Be awake. Be alive. BE THE LOVE.

Something totally New is coming into our relationships. . .

Absolutely new forms of relationship are in the process of being born. None of us yet knows exactly what they are, but we can feel it. And we certainly have a good idea of what they are not. These new forms of relationship will be emphasized in our lives once the Third Gate is activated in 1997, for this is what Third Gate is all about. They will be totally different than anything we have experienced before. The New Relationship model will be greatly expanded, more all-inclusive than our previous one. We will no longer be limited to loving just one being.

Already many of us are facing the dilemma of being in love with more than one person. What to do? How do we choose between two strong loves? How do we act with integrity and not fall into old patterns? The reason these situations are happening is to stretch our Love wider, to be more All-Encompassing. Our challenge is to keep our Love open to everyone. This doesn't mean that we have to be physically intimate, but we should be able to love whole-heartedly without threatening our existing relationships.

Our Love will be emanating from such a clear, clean place that everyone will feel the full force of our Love. Remember: the One Heart is a vast reservoir of Love. There's a limitless supply of Love for everyone. Our process of discovery has just begun.

• Making Love in the Invisible •

Our approach to sexuality will also be vastly transformed. The New Partnerships are wide open, stripped to the core, passionate, vulnerable, openhearted and surprisingly comforting. We can hold nothing back, nor do we want to. We come together in Love, trust, openness, mutual support and respect. As we become integrated Earth-Star Beings, we will be more Vibrantly Alive than ever before. We will love passionately, wildly, purely, deeply, more intimately than we've ever imagined possible. Making Love with the full depth of our beings—from Earth to Star.

It's a strange paradox, but as we become increasingly vaster and more alive, we find that we are more open and vulnerable than ever before. Yet, there's a tremendous strength in this vulnerability. We love more intimately, yet are more detached. This new sense of detachment is based on our interwoven Oneness with everything. We can deeply love one tiny aspect of the One, but at the same time, we are always part of the larger One. This gives us a huge perspective which always takes us to a vaster vantage point. So by embracing one person, we are embracing all beings. How this will affect our sexuality is that our emphasis will shift from the physical levels of making love to new ways of making love with our full beings in the Spaces-in-Between. We will be making Love in the subtle realms of the Invisible.

The emphasis of our lovemaking will shift from the physical arena, currently centered in our sexual organs, to an infinitely vaster sphere. Lovemaking will still be felt in the physical, but not be limited to it. We will experience the sensations of making Love not only in our physical bodies, but in our vaster subtle bodies as well. This expansion will further serve to liberate us from duality.

• How to LOVE LARGE •

An Initiation for Men:

For men to make this shift, it entails a powerful initiation called the Greater Phallus. They must release their attachment to their physical phallus and let their whole being become the Greater Phallus. When you make Love, do it with your Greater Phallus. See your entire physical body as a huge phallus. When you really feel this activate, there will be a throbbing sensation of vibrant aliveness which fills you with powerful sensations. Now, go even further and embrace your full vastness— from core of Earth to core of Star. This is your larger body. It is your Greater Phallus and this is what you make Love with. Try this and discover the massive difference it makes. It is a mammoth quantum leap in lovemaking and the key to Loving Large on a small planet.

An Initiation for Women:

As men embody their Greater Phallus, women must prepare themselves to meet them on a similar level. Otherwise, you will not be able to experience true Sacred Union. Imagine trying to make love between a man who has activated his Greater Phallus and a woman who is still embodying her duality-based personality self. It would not only be unfulfilling; it would be a disaster! The same is true of a woman who has embraced her vastness and desires to make Love with her full being who tries to make love with a man who is only focused on his physical genitals.

Making Love is Sacred Union.

To experience true Sacred Union while making Love it definitely helps if you pick a partner who is on the same level of awareness as you. This is vitally important. It's also important to genuinely love the other person. If you don't, why are you making Love? If you're simply motivated by lust, then you are still bogged down in duality. Or perhaps you are afraid of true intimacy, letting someone touch the core of your being. Sure, it's sometimes messy and always scary, but so what! Anything real is powerful and challenging. If we don't risk stretching our comfortable old parameters, if we are afraid of truly being touched or the profound depth of our emotions, then we will never know what it is to be fully, Vibrantly Alive!

THE EIGHTEENTH KEY:

All-Encompassing Sacred Union

All-Encompassing Sacred Union. . .

We all want more Love in our lives.

We often define this yearning for love as the longing for a special partner. While it would be wonderful to have a fulfilling, love relationship, we are rather limiting ourselves by thinking that this is the major mode for love to express itself in our lives.

Sacred Union is our most natural state of being.

Sacred Union is all around us every single moment. It surrounds and embraces us, if only we would see it. Look around you and you will be amazed at the profusion of Sacred Union constantly taking place. The Sun is making love with the sky. The sky is making love with the Earth. The Earth is making love with the plants. The wind is making love with the trees. The sea makes love with the shore. That's what nature truly is, a wide panorama of Love. If you can allow yourselves to feel it, you too, will be embraced in All-Encompassing Sacred Union.

Love's journey through biology.

We can look upon our entire biological evolutionary journey on this Earth and see this process of Sacred Union. It began with the creation of this planet. What an act of Love!

Then biological life began with the single celled creatures making love with themselves. Everything on Gaia is so intricately and intimately woven together, so interdependent on each other—all acts of Making Love. In spite of outer appearances, this is a planet of Love.

We are Making Love all the time.

Now you are probably thinking that I've gone too far. But stay with me for a few minutes longer. Sit quietly while you read this. Be very still. Now feel the air upon your face. . . That's right, it's touching you, isn't it? Actually, it's caressing you right now. Allow yourself to feel it. The air upon your skin. Sweetly, subtly loving you. . . Very good. What about your clothes? Can you feel them touching you? They are in love with your skin. Feel their Sacred Union.

Now turn your attention to your body and your chair. What are they doing? That's right, more Sacred Union. Feel how the chair loves supporting your body and how much your body is grateful to be supported. How comfortably they melt into each other. Place your feet upon the floor and feel how the floor rises up to greet your feet as gravity pulls your feet to the floor. Sacred Union strikes again!

Very slowly, I'd like you to stand up and allow that sense of Sacred Union to increase. Feel the air all around you, delicately caressing you. Carefully walk across the room. With each step, feel the Sacred Union between your feet and the floor, your skin and the air, your clothes and your skin. This is All-Encompassing Sacred Union and it's always been here. We were just too busy to feel it before.

Start noticing all the myriad ways Sacred Union is taking place all the time. Drink a glass of water and feel the liquid

Love melting inside you. The next time that it rains, go outside and experience Sacred Union with the rain. Watch those drops of water on the leaves of plants and see what's really happening! They're making Love. Go swimming and get the full effect. Or lie in the sun and feel it kissing you all over.

This is just a taste of the Greater Love which is now being revealed. You might think that I'm being silly, but just go try it! Then you'll understand. Open yourself up to Love; it's always all around you. So if you used to think that you were alone, now try being All-One.

Of course, this only works if you are quiet and still enough to feel the subtle energies. If your mind is going five thousand miles a minute with agitated thoughts, or if you haven't tuned into the waves of the Invisible, you probably won't feel anything. Ah, but if you do, you'll discover that there's a whole world of Sacred Union happening all the time. You can enter this magical realm of Love and live the rest of your life there if you wish. And it will only get stronger.

THE NINETEENTH KEY:

Integrating the Impossible

Integrating the Impossible. . .

Heightened Experiences become our Future Foundations.

Continually expanding our beings brings to us a new challenge, that of Integrating the Impossible. Each time that we travel deeper into the Invisible, we must return back to our starting point, only to discover that this too, has undergone a startling transformation. Our very foundation has shifted and we can no longer go back to our old bottom line. As we become increasingly vaster, our foundation always rises to a new level.

This is because we are traveling on a two way journey. Not only do we go into the Invisible, but our task is to bring the Invisible here, anchoring it into the physical. Remember, we are now Earth-Star beings. This means that all the polarities have merged into Oneness inside our beings. There's no more separation between spirit and matter, between Earth and Star. There is only the One.

Our process of expansion is much like blowing up a balloon. When there are heightened energies about, when the surf is up, we fill our balloons bigger than they have ever been before. It feels so exhilarating and liberating to be this expansive and free. Then we try to return back to our previous conditions, only to find that everything has changed. This is because we have so transformed, our vibrations have quickened, irrevocably altering the old harmonics.

This expansion into a heightened reality followed by a thud back into our previous reality system creates a profound state of insecurity, for our old props have grown wobbly indeed. What do we do now? Rising panic sets in as we feel the air rushing out of our expanded balloons. Well, what do we do? Quick, we have to do something or we will Null Zone!

At this point, there are several courses of action we can take:

• Hold Onto Everything for Dear Life! •

This is a very popular response to our feelings of insecurity and raw vulnerability. Since we've been propelled into the Unknown which makes us *very, very* uncomfortable, *(That's why it's called the Unknown.)* we decide to grab onto everything we can from our old belief systems. Tenaciously holding onto them more tightly than ever before. This we try to justify by repeating loudly to ourselves and anyone who might be looking at us questioningly, *"Look, this is what I know; this is what I do well. We've got to get back to reality; we can't live our lives in the clouds, you know. My life's perfect the way it is. I don't have to make any changes."* The *same old, same old* has never looked so good or felt so comforting.

And then what happens? We start living a lie, pretending that we are small beings. Now this ruse might fool some people, especially those who have a vested interest in your remaining your old self, but it certainly won't fool you! And how are you going to live with yourself? Things might work out OK for a while, but sooner or later you're going to come crashing head-on with that huge part of your Greater Self which you're keeping locked up in denial. This is not a pretty sight and causes a lot of unnecessary pain.

• Pop Goes the Balloon •

In this possible scenario, we return home and discover that our previous reality wasn't real! We were living a fake life in an unreal world. This causes such an immense shock that the balloon of our expansion is popped. We begin to Null Zone and all our worlds start crashing down upon us. Now this isn't quite as bad as it sounds; at least we're not in denial. Of course, it could have been avoided if we hadn't let go of our balloon so quickly, if we'd had more confidence and trust in ourselves and in the waves of the Invisible.

What do you do now? First, look at your Null Zone and accept it. Don't try to pick up the pieces of your old life and put them back together. You couldn't anyway. Now honor your Null Zone as an important process in your life, for it creates the womb of the New. Perhaps, this would be a most appropriate time to make a massive surrender of the *Past That Never Was*. And then, turn your full attention to birthing your New Self.

• Lifting That Bottom Line •

Here's a third possibility. When you return home and discover that nothing is the same as it was before, simply accept it. Isn't that what transformation is all about? Didn't we ask for a quantum leap? Accept that the Unknown is presently unknowable. Accept that you have been catapulted into a new level of awareness. As you find that you don't fit back into all the aspects of your former life, don't try to. It's good to be different than you were before. Weed through your old life and get rid of everything which no longer resonates with the Highest Truth of your Core Self. Clean out those closets. Let go of or transform those old relationships. Allow your previous security systems to be dissolved.

No matter what, keep on honoring your newly expanded being. It's fine to be vulnerable and undefined. So what, if you don't know anything anymore! Stay wide open, tender, so very vulnerable. Stay with it until it becomes comfortable. Keep your Love flowing. There's a great freedom coming, and a new life about to be born.

As you do this, you will make the truth of your expansion your own, and a deep integration will take place within the core of your being, merging into each cell of your body. Then watch as your bottom line rises and a new foundation is created. This is how we integrate the impossible.

THE TWENTIETH KEY:

Star Language

Star Language...

Ana-lita ki-yano kima ca'i:
Star Language is the language of the Invisible.

All of us have the inherent ability to speak Star Languages; they are our original tongues. Using Star Language is actually a far more natural way of expression than our earthly languages. With Star Language, we can speak the unspoken. We can communicate from the core of our beings. We can effortlessly express what we don't yet know that we know.

There are myriad dialects of Star Language, just as there are myriad star systems. Although we can each speak several dialects, we also have the amazing ability to understand any Star Language we hear. Star Language is not understood by the mind. Rather, it is transmitted directly into our cells where it activates the appropriate sectors of our cellular memory banks. We understand it with our hearts. There is no word-to-word translation, for this would be way too limiting. Instead, there is a transference of essence, each sound expressing far more meaning than we can presently perceive. Each word of Star Language is like the corner of a hologram, revealing a vast universe of meaning.

This also means that we don't have to undergo the arduous process of memorizing Star Language. It is a fluid, alive, always changing, mode of communication. Whatever Star

Language I have used in this Key is simply for the purpose of illustrating some possible sounds of one of my dialects, and is not meant to be memorized or taken as the only way of expressing those phrases in Star Language. There are no fixed definitions assigned to the sounds of Star Language. It has more to do with the alignment of Core Essence to sound frequencies within the matrix of Oneness. By aligning ourselves to the waves of the Invisible, we can open ourselves up to new universes of expression.

Starry Names Ay•Ki•Na•Ma:

Another aspect of Star Language is our Starry Name. Starry Names originate from the Template of Oneness and express our Core Essence. They are not anchored in duality like our old earthly names, nor do they have karmic histories. Think about what we carry around with us when we are named after our cranky old Aunt Edna, or something like John Randolph III or Caesar Elvis Augustus Smith. We not only have to deal with our karma, but everyone else who has used that name as well. Even our surname brings with it all that family's old karmic patternings. It's another very good reason to use our Starry Names and step beyond the realms of duality.

The first Starry Names which we received denoted our various star lineages and were often quite long. Many of us now use these names all the time. They set up a vibrational patterning within us of openness, freedom, Oneness and the One Heart. As we travel deeper into the Invisible, we are discovering that even these Starry Names are beginning to change. Many are already receiving new Starry Names which are deeper, much shorter and extremely simple. They are almost root sounds and originate from a far vaster place than our original Starry Names.

Eta ki-yano kivé ma:

Many of the ancient root languages of this planet still contain the seeds of Star Language. Although now assigned specific meanings, the words of ancient tongues have a natural resonance which expands their current definition. The sounds of these ancient root words naturally trigger worlds of remembrance. It's also interesting to note the stunning similarity of root words in many languages of the world. This is because they all originated from Star Languages.

Here's an example of a few meanings of the word TAWA.
Tibetan: *Moon*
Hopi: *Sun*
Quechua (the Inca language): *the sacred number four.*
Afghani: *one who folds clothes.*
Balinese: *one who bargains in the marketplace.*
Hindi: *the cauldron, a cooking pot.*

Here's the word NANI:
Tibetan: *daughter*
Hindi: *grandmother*
Hawaiian: *beautiful*
Nahuatl (the Mayan language): *the sacred number four.*
Quechua: *clarity.*

As we step into our vastness, it's important that we create larger and deeper methods of expression. Using Star Language gives us a new form of communication which enables us to naturally express our vastness. And it's quite easy to learn since we already know it. We learned Star Language before we ever came to this planet. All we have to do is dive in and let it come out!

It's tremendously liberating to allow ourselves to speak Star Language. Finally, we are given an avenue to express what has been so long dammed up inside our depths. Often, when we first speak Star Language there is a huge outburst of joy and laughter. We feel so free! Star Language is profound and tender, *frequently hilarious*, always deeply sacred, and so much fun. And now when we meet our Starry Family from other countries, we don't have to translate our conversations into various earthly languages; we can all speak in our various dialects of Star Language and be understood by all.

• Practical Applications of Star Language •

Here's a somewhat playful, but true, guided tour through some of the very practical ways you can use Star Language in your everyday life:

• Business Meetings •

Let's dive right in to what many would consider an unlikely arena for using Star Language, the world of business. How many boring business meetings have we endured? Well, no more! I've enlivened many "serious" business meetings by beginning my presentation with Star Language. This has instantly recalibrated the energy and put the meeting on a new track. It certainly pulls the rug out from under people's egos and lets them know right away that we are dealing with a Greater Reality. Be daring and try it!

• Problem Solving •

Got a problem? Well, don't waste time sitting around and discussing it in your normal language. Instead, try Star Language. The clarity of its resonance will cut through to the core, without the anxieties, worries and emotional distortions of duality. After a little discussion in Star Language, the natural solution to your problem will be revealed.

• Relationships •

Do you have trouble communicating intimately with your mate? Are there lots of feelings buried deep inside you which you'd like to express? Have no fear, Star Language is here! Just plunge in with Star Language and you will find that it flings open new doors of communication, taking your relationship to unimagined depths. Star Language is unbelievably passionate and tender. Try expressing your Love to each other with it, and see what happens!

I've even performed a rather unique Star Language marriage ceremony in Germany. This was somewhat challenging since it was the first marriage ceremony I had ever done and I had absolutely no idea what to do. My nervousness heightened when I discovered that the couple getting married just had a big argument and weren't speaking to each other. But, as usual, Star Language came to the rescue. . .

To begin, I had everyone get in a big circle and do the Lotus Dance. Then I placed the wedding couple who were very sweet, though glaring fiercely at each other, in the center of our dance. They sat on the floor, facing one another and I covered them with a big cloth. (Actually, it was a magenta pareo from Tahiti with a shell fringe. Quite nice.) Then I told them to express their true feelings to their partner in Star Language.

The rest of us held the Beam while doing the Lotus Dance for what seemed like aeons. We encircled them with Love and listened to a raging torrent of Star Language from under the cloth. We continued to hold the Beam and kept on dancing. The petals of the Lotus breathed in and out while Star Language continued under the protection of that cloth, but I could sense that the problems were being resolved. Finally, the tone of the Star Language sweetened and deepened and by the time the cloth was removed, they had returned to Oneness and their marriage had taken place. Then Omashar played, *Spiral Through The Stars* and we all danced with abandon. It was a perfect wedding!

• With Children •

Star Language is one of the deepest ways we can communicate with children. They absolutely love it and jump into full fluency with no effort at all. Although it's always preferable to start immersing them into the Greater Reality at birth, before they pick up any of duality's bad habits, Star Language can be introduced at any age. It's fun and it's effective. So if you're tired of dealing with unruly or rebellious children, especially those highly empowered Starchildren, pull out your secret weapon—Star Language, and watch your communications improve!

• With Other Species •

Living creatures adore being talked to in Star Language. They know that we are communicating on a deeper level, from essence to essence in the One Heart. You can begin by practicing with domestic animals such as the pets in your household. Instead of going, "Here, doggy, doggy," try something like, "Ki-e-neh, koosh-ne." This is sure to get a response and usually wins a lot more respect from your furry friend. *A word of warning: Please, don't try this phrase on cats!*

Now you are ready to go outside and practice on something bigger, like a horse, cow or elephant. They perked right up when you spoke to them in Star Language, didn't they? I once knew a dairy farmer who had great success Star Aligning his cows. And after he began speaking to them in Star Language, their milk production greatly increased.

The next step is to go talk to some birds or other wild creatures. When you do, you'll discover that they don't run away. In fact, they often come closer and listen to you more carefully, with their ears perked up and their heads cocked from side to side. I tell you, they all *love* Star Language. And just think what meaningful conversations you can have. You can express your deepest Love, and tell them about how we are moving from duality to Oneness and to spread the word to the rest of their species.

Living creatures all have a sort of chief archetype which we call the Deva of the species. All members of that species are directly linked in with their Deva. This Deva is not really a personified being, but rather a personified master archetype of that particular species. So if you ever have problems with a specific creature, such as mice in your house, overbearing insects, etc., it is often more effective to deal directly with the Deva.

This can lead to numerous, unexpected adventures. I won't delve into my own personal stories at this time, but will merely add a warning about the Scorpion Deva. If you ever encounter this formidable being, *and you should probably try not to—unless there's an urgent need,* you will never forget it. I've heard similar comments about the Rat Deva. Anyway, not to digress, whenever you do need to deal with the Deva of a particular species, you will meet much greater success, and obtain more respect, if you use Star Language.

• Rocks, plants, oceans, mountains, etc. •

The next time that you are outside, try speaking in Star Language to the rocks, mountains and hills. They will understand you as never before. The same is true of oceans, rivers and lakes. Sing to them in Starry Language and it gets even better! Don't worry if you're not a good singer; *everyone's a great singer in Star Language.* Now go into a forest and sing to the trees. Watch very carefully and you will see their leaves swaying in response. All of nature is hungry for real communication. Often, we forget this and go blithely on our way without acknowledging the Presence of the great nature beings who surround us.

Then there's the matter of plants. Try talking to your house plants and your garden in Star Language. Sing to them and shower them with your Love. They'll grow much happier and have a greater production if you do. Flowers especially love being complimented on their beauty. When we speak with other species in Star Language, we are acknowledging our conscious connection with them—that we are all interwoven into Oneness.

• Man-made objects •

Man-made objects also respond well to Star Language. This includes cars, computers, tools and cooking utensils. They will all work with you more harmoniously if you communicate with them. Each of them has their own life-force as well as unique personality. It's extremely worthwhile to make friends with the objects which you use on a daily basis. It will make a huge difference if you are loving allies, working together as One Being. It will also increase the Love around you.

• The Creative Process •

Star Language greatly empowers and intensifies the creative process. I often sing in Star Language while making paintings. This not only increases my focus, but brings what I do to a deeper level. Many singers have discovered that if they sing in Star Language, much more can be expressed. And whether you consider yourself a singer or not, singing in Star Language takes you to a deeper level. *Everyone* can sing in Star Language.

• Healing •

If you are a healer, try using Star Language in your next session and see what happens! Teach it to your clients and it will help them open the doors to their Core Self. This will immeasurably enhance whatever process you are doing.

• Remembering •

With Star Language we can express many things that were previously impossible to articulate. It is a great tool to access the knowledge stored within our cellular memory banks—to remember what we didn't know that we knew. When you need to remember something, the memory which lies dormant within you will come out easily.

Another fun thing to do is telling stories in Star Language with a group of your friends. Sit in a circle and begin the story. When the first person stops, the next person takes up the story where it left off. And on around the circle. You can recount the entire history of the planet in this manner, delineate your next step, or tell funny stories.

• Heightened Spiritual Experiences •

Use Star Language in your prayers and ceremonies. You can also evoke one of the Starry Councils. Star Language will be purer and infinitely more powerful than even the most ancient earthly languages. It will evoke the Greater Reality and take you deeper into the Invisible.

• •

By now, you should be bursting with enthusiasm to try speaking Star Language. You can do it right now. Just set aside your mind, open your mouth, and let the sounds come forth. Please, don't worry about how they're going to sound. Some dialects of Star Language sound very weird, others are hilarious and some are exquisitely beautiful. It really doesn't matter. The important thing is to get started.

Here's a practice you can do to polish up your fluency in Star Language:

• Spinner Wheels: Ki•Yo•Toh•Ko •

This process is most effective with a small group of people, but you can also try it by yourself. If you have a large group, form several Spinner Wheels with seven or eight people per wheel. The idea is that we're going to form a wheel of energy and then we'll start spinning this wheel faster and faster until it takes off. Sit in a circle, quite close together, but not touching. If you're sitting in chairs, place your feet firmly on the floor in the Sitting GO position. Make sure that your legs are uncrossed and your hands are placed palms down upon your legs. *Warning:* At times, this practice can get quite hilarious, so stay firmly anchored in the Sitting GO.

Choose someone in your group to be the anchor of your Spinner Wheel. They will begin each round, followed by the person to their left and on around the circle in a clockwise fashion. When everyone is finished, open up into the One Heart. Try to align yourselves into One Being so that all your arms upraise at the same time. Feel your One Being intensify each time you do this. When you are ready to begin the next round, lower your hands and place them back upon your legs in the Sitting GO position.

For the first two rounds *only*, we're going to keep going around the circle several times, very quickly, until the anchor-person feels that it's time to stop. Each time that it is your turn speak quickly, without thinking about what you're going to say. This will help activate the Spinner Wheel. Beginning with Round Three, we will only go around the circle once, followed by our movements into the One Heart.

Remember: Spinner Wheels are not done with our minds, so please set your mind aside until we are finished. Using Star Language, we can speak the unspoken.

Round One:
Make a quick short sound. *(Examples: eh, uh, ho, eep, etc.)* Go around your circle faster and faster, making the energy spin.

Round Two:
Say something brief and funny in Star Language. Keep go-

ing around faster and faster, spinning your wheel until the anchor tells you to stop.

Round Three:

Speaking only in Star Language, tell us who you really are. *When everyone has spoken, open into the One Heart.*

Round Four:

Why did you come to Earth? What is your purpose here? *Then into the One Heart.*

Round Five:

Now speak to your Truest Beloved, telling them everything you have ever wanted to say. *Do not personify your Beloved into a specific person.*

Round Six:

What is your next step?

Round Seven:

What are your keywords for this year?

Round Eight:

Now speak some words in Star Language which will clear your path into the future. *This part can be very powerful. As you do this, feel the shift in energy. You will feel an opening outwards in front of you. Often you will receive revelations about your future; so be extra alert.*

Round Nine:

Sing in Star Language to the planet and all the living beings upon her. Sing to them of the vast Love in the One

Heart. And as you sing, feel a great healing taking place, a melting away of duality. *As the songs finish, go back into the One Heart and hold the energy.*

That's it. It really isn't difficult to learn to speak our real languages. And it feels tremendously liberating! You can add other rounds to this process of whatever you want to express. Spinner Wheels are a great way to align a group of people into Oneness and make major breakthroughs into Star Language fluency.

THE TWENTY-FIRST KEY:

Our
Core Selves

Our Core Selves. . .

Stripped to the Core:

To travel deeper into the Invisible, we must find our Core Self. This is who we really are without all the myriad decorations, assumed roles, disguises, without our personalities, established habits or preferences. *Our true, no frills Essence.* This basic, no frills version of our Self comes without all the attractive add-ons of cleverness, beauty, knowledge, experience, acquired skills, charm, etc. Our Core Self is stripped down, raw, true, vulnerable, tender. Sounds fun, doesn't it? Well, it's not so bad once we get there. Possibly a bit uncomfortable until we get used to it, but critically important.

How to we find our Core Self? One of the fastest ways is to undergo some sort of crisis which forces us to forego our old patterns and personality, enabling us to access our untapped, long hidden reservoirs of courage, strength and depth. A crisis always sorts out what's real and what's illusion rather quickly. Another method is to engage in a dramatic, passionate relationship—the kind which strips you bare and flings you down in the dust. Or you could partake in an engrossing creative endeavour in which you focus your whole being. Find some activity which takes everything you've got. Give it everything, then stretch beyond that and give it more. A powerful spiritual experience will also strip you down to your Core Self.

Since we may not be presented with a convenient crisis, dramatic relationship, heightened spiritual experience or creative endeavour when we need one to find our Core Self, we'll look for other ways to strip ourselves down to the bare essentials. To do this, we need to clear out most of the distractions which take up our attention. An easy way is to go on a retreat. Take a long hike or go somewhere quiet by yourself and leave your personality behind. Have a vacation from your usual self and discover who's really there. If you can't just take off, you can also do this at home by creating a zone of safety or Neutral Zone.

Slowly strip away the various levels of superficial personality which you have acquired. Go ahead and carefully dismantle your being. Take off everything that defines you. Keep shedding each layer as it reveals itself. It's like gently peeling an onion. Take it one layer at a time. Be very, very conscious about everything you do. Take off all of the roles you've acquired, all those outer personas. Let go of all your *shoulds* and *supposed to's*. Stop *trying* and start doing. Stop *hoping* and start manifesting. Only do what your heart prompts you to do. This is the One Heart; don't follow the whims and desires of your smaller heart. Be real. Be true. This means no more little lies or half truths. No more unconscious, preprogrammed responses. Constantly recenter your being back into your core.

At this point, you might encounter your internal judge and jury. That's the part of you which is constantly making pronouncements: *"You're not good enough!" "You're not smart enough!" "You're lazy & good for nothing!" "You're too fat/ thin, young/old, slow/fast!" "You don't deserve Love!" "You're not beautiful enough!" "Guilty, guilty, guilty!"* OK, OK, that's enough! Don't even try to deal with your judge; don't worry about trying to present your case. It doesn't really matter whether you are or aren't any of these things. Just let them babble on and strip off another layer. Keep going until even the judge and jury are stripped off too.

The closer we get to our Core Selves, the more awkward and uncomfortable it will feel. This discomfort and sense of awkwardness comes from the stripping off of our comfy, highly esteemed frills and from our heightened vulnerability. Our Core Self is so very raw and tender that often when we find it, we want to cover it up and flee as fast as possible. This is an old preprogrammed response. Please resist this urge and stay with it. Fortunately, our Core Self contains a vast storehouse of courage. Find your inner bedrock of courage and pull it out. Stay with it. Learn to live wide open, raw, stripped and vulnerable.

Another thing we should watch out for is the inevitable padding of our Core Self. This happens even if we are fully committed to staying open. Subtle layers of preferences, assumptions, outer roles, personality and attitudes will slowly, almost imperceptibly, attach themselves to your Core Self. Be alert for this and keep shedding your skins until you're back to your Core.

It is this Core Self who will lead us into our new lives. We really need it in order to birth our New Selves and become fully alive. Once you find your Core Self, anchor your being there. Let it be the part of you which predominates. Whenever you find yourself covering up your Core Self, start stripping off the layers until you reach it again. Then remain there for as long as possible. Eventually, it will become surprisingly comfortable to be raw, true, stripped, wide open and vulnerable. You will find a tremendous strength in this. It anchors us in a new depth of raw Truth. We have finally become real.

• Living in Our Core Self •

Once we reconnect with our Core Self, we will discover many changes in our life. Everything we do will emanate a deeper resonance of truth. While this may be occasionally shocking, it will ultimately be profoundly fulfilling. Look at how long we kept our deepest truths locked up inside ourselves or watered them down so we could attempt to be well liked. You will discover a tremendous sense of relief when everything you do reflects your deepest truth. You can finally live your life without compromise!

If you're still concerned that this is going to put a crimp in your popularity, then simply let go of your attachment to being popular. The people who really count in your life will respect you more if you are real, even if you are raw, stripped and vulnerable! In my own life experiences I have found that there are always people who don't like me, no matter how hard I try to please them or accommodate myself to their needs. I have learned to let these people go and get on with my real business of being true to myself. *BE REAL, no matter what!*

If you are motivated by your Core Self, you will be able to achieve clear actions without having to prove yourself to others. You won't have to "build a case" to create a method of propulsion. So many people feel the need to conjure up numerous excuses and justifications for their actions when they are doing something out of balance with their Core Self. They fabricate a false scenario which helps cover over their walls of denial. All of this is simply because they are not listening to their Core Self. You can save yourself lots of trouble and heartache if you constantly acknowledge your Core Self. It will provide you with all the natural motivation you need.

Your Core Self is the Seed Core of your New Being.

Your Core Self is one of the truest friends you have. Learn to trust it; it will not lead you astray. After awhile, you will love this new feeling of heightened truth, of stripped down aliveness. You will be grateful to be freed of the layers of petty superficialities. You will love feeling more alert, awake and alive. And now that you have uncovered the seed core of your New Being, the birth process can intensify.

Living

on a small planet

does not mean

that WE
have to be small.

THE TWENTY-SECOND KEY:

How To Live Large

How to Live Large. . .

Living Large is a state of being.

Once we have made our commitment to embrace our vastness, we must be prepared to go the distance. This ever increasing sense of vastness must be constantly and diligently anchored into the physical. It is something we do on a daily basis. We do it wherever we are, regardless of what we are doing. It is a process of continual wakefulness, being ever alert, remaining in touch with our Core Selves and never forgetting who we are. This is how we establish the New Normal, a heightened state of awareness in which our very foundation is profoundly transformed.

We are awakening from our final dream into the Greater Reality.

Living Large is the big wake up, the stepping free from our illusory dream state of being partially alive. We are finally on the road to becoming Vibrantly Alive! And just think about it. How many people have ever been truly alive? Most of us on this planet have spent our entire cycle of incarnations in a hazy dream state, flitting from one illusion to the next. Using only one tenth of our brain on our best days. Trying to love with our pathetically puny small hearts and warped third dimensional personalities. Locked into our narrow old behavior patterns like unthinking robots. No wonder life hasn't made much sense or been fulfilling.

If you're ready to experience something totally New, if you want to shake off your slumber and truly WAKE UP and become Vibrantly Alive, if you want your very cells to be quickened into the frequencies of Ecstatic Love, then it's time to Master the Art of Living Large.

• Mastering the Art of Living Large •

Many of us are discontented with our current life situations. If only we could move, change careers, make more money, have a new relationship. We are bristling with impatience to change our outer world. Well, here's the key you seek:

We must first transform ourselves before we can expect our outer world to change.

Remember that the physical is the last place the Greater Reality manifests. In order to embody these heightened frequencies and anchor them into the physical world around us, we must first do it within ourselves. Otherwise, right now we could be given a new job, new location, more money and a new relationship, and everything would remain the same. We would still maintain the same habits, patterns, attitudes, limited spiritual concepts, imbalances and duality based personas. Deep fulfillment would continue to elude us.

At this point, it is far preferable not to focus on the outer changes you desire, for that will only increase your impatience and frustration. Instead, turn your attention back to yourself. Let's focus on learning to Live Large on this small planet. If we can do this, we will soon birth our New Selves. It is these New Selves who are going to live our new lives. Once they are born, just watch and see how quickly your outer world will rearrange itself to more perfectly support your New Self. This transformation will be effortless and unquestionable.

• Expansive Acceptance •

We can begin by letting go of our old preferences. Instead, move into a state of wide, expanded acceptance. This isn't that old, wimpy passive acceptance of *"Oh well, whatever happens, happens."* Nor is it a state of resigned compromise. Rather it is an all-encompassing embrace of the current conditions in your life *from a vantage point of vastness.* Know that all the elements in your life are here for a reason; they all have a gift to give you. Find the lesson inherent in each situation, learn it, and move on. This will give you an expansive acceptance that will actually serve to loosen and transform the boundaries around you. It will also help you look at everything with new eyes.

• The Philosopher's Stone •

Here's the secret of the alchemists revealed. Do you want to turn lead into gold? It's easier than you imagine. What's the secret? Turning lead into gold refers to transmuting denser energies into heightened frequencies of Light. Let's look at the concept of negativity. First of all, negativity only exists within the Template of Duality. That's where we enact the continuous dramas between dark and light. It's the realm of the Dark and Light Lords with their constant battle for supremacy and control.

Now, let's step into the Template of Oneness. Here, there is no more negativity, no more forces of evil. The One is All-Encompassing; everything is part of the One. From this much wider vantage point we are able to see the inherent perfection in everything. We can see that so-called negative energy is actually serving a Higher Purpose. All of it, even the things that we don't yet understand. When we anchor ourselves in Oneness, we become freed of the concept of negativity. Guess what this does to us! It further unhooks us from duality, and negativity loses its power. Thus we transform lead into gold.

• Helpful Hints •
• for the Time of Completion •

Cleanliness is Godliness:

It's important that we keep ourselves and our surroundings in a state of cleanliness and order. This isn't just for the sake of neatness, but it's to establish clarity and create a Neutral Zone in which we can explore the Invisible.

How Clean Are You?

When we are in the midst of constantly recalibrating our energies; it's vitally important that we remain aware of the state of our physical body. Great changes are taking place within this temple of ours and there is much that we can do to aid the process.

Purification:
The first step is Purification. Now we're not talking about extreme measures here, but simply being aware of the small things we can do to help keep our energies balanced and flowing. If we wash our bodies regularly, we're not just washing away the dirt; we're cleansing our energy. So, take showers and baths often. Whenever you do, remain conscious that you are also clearing your energy. When there is intense energy around, I often take two or three showers a day. The same is true when something upsetting happens. As soon as possible, take a shower and wash that discordant energy away.

The Waterfall:
If you're feeling a lack of Love in your life, then step under your waterfall, *(that trusty old shower)* and feel yourself being drenched in liquid Love. Let Love melt into you. Fill yourself with Love. You'll come out refreshed and renewed.

Take a Power Shower:
This is for those in a hurry—when you're exhausted, have only a few free minutes and have to keep going. It takes less than five minutes including dressing time. Jump into your shower and face the water spray. Now lift your hands up to the water and with a great whooshing noise bring your arms down your front and out to your sides. Whoosh off that old energy. Then turn to your right so your left side is facing the water and repeat the process. Do this three more times, with your back facing the water, then your right side, and your front again. Now jump out of your Power Shower. You'll be amazed at how much better you feel.

The Splash:

The Splash is a great technique for cleansing our energies when we are out in the world. It is even quicker than the Power Shower. Go to any water supply: a faucet, glass of water, stream, whatever is handy. Dab your fingertips in the water and put water at the inner edge of your eyes, then the outer edge. Throw some water on your forehead and wash it over your temples. Splash some more water on the rest of your face, starting at your mouth and working outwards. If you have extra time, put water on your neck, especially the back of your neck, and behind your ears. Now wash your hands and splash water on the inside of your wrists, a most important spot. You might want to toss a little water on your heart. There, you've been totally renewed! The Splash Technique really works. I often do it 8-10 times a day, especially when I'm out in the wild world.

We're not Camels:

That's right, we're not camels, so let's come out of the desert. There is plentiful water to drink, so let's drink it. OFTEN. It's essential that we drink lots and lots of water. This helps rid our body of toxins, and we've all got lots of toxins just waiting to be released. And while you're on your tenth glass of water, please remember to drink it consciously. This is Sacred Union taking place, remember? Fill your body regularly with liquid Love and feel it melt into you. If water gets too boring after your fiftieth glass, try adding a splash of juice or making herbal iced tea. But keep drinking!

Tiger Balm:

Tiger Balm is an inexpensive Chinese salve which is full of powerful ingredients like camphor and eucalyptus. It can be purchased worldwide in Chinese stores or health food shops. It has practically saved my life on numerous occasions, and I always carry some with me. It is highly recommended whenever you get zapped with duality: things like astral and psychic bombardment, third eye zap from another person, and times of great emotional disturbance. Whenever necessary, dab some Tiger Balm on your forehead and temples, and on your neck under your ears. Be careful not to get it into your eyes. The effect will be simultaneously hot and cold; when it abates, your energy will be clear.

• Loving Your Body •

Our physical bodies are tremendously responsive to Love. This is obvious when we're in a relationship. We love being loved. But Love isn't limited to the presence of another person; we need to learn to love and honor our bodies all the time. We can begin with expanded acceptance. Look at your body and accept it just the way it is right now, with all its perceived imperfections. Our physical forms are wondrous instruments and they are quite capable of constantly transforming themselves into ever greater perfection. But first we must love them in their present state.

How do you treat your body? Do you just stuff it into clothes like a sausage each morning? Is your skin all dry and scaly due to neglect? Are you ashamed of your body? If so, there's work to be done. But don't worry; it's going to be fun. Go out and buy some beautiful lotion or scented oil. Don't just slap it on, but caress it into your skin. Keep telling your body how much you love it; how grateful you are to live in it. If this sounds too embarrassing, speak to it in Star Language. Physical bodies *love* Star Language. Find special ways that you can honor your body. Treat it to a bubble bath or a massage. You'll notice right away how it starts to perk up.

Physical bodies love to be used. They exult in all forms of exercise and play. So check and see if you're giving your body enough to do. Are you playing with it regularly? Bodies are somewhat like dogs in this respect, they need not only food and water, but they require being taken on frequent walks and good playful romps. So if your body was a dog, what would he be doing? If your dog is over in the corner whimpering weakly, then it's time to pay him some quality attention. Take him out for a frisky adventure or dance up a storm in your room. You'll both have lots of fun. And you can't Live Large unless you're having fun!

Of course, there are some people who pay too much attention to their bodies. They are constantly fussing over them, to the exclusion of much else. They feel that if their hair is perfect or their muscles are well defined, that this validates them as worthy beings. However, there's an imbalance here, an overcompensation for something that's missing inside.

If this is your case, then we would suggest that you allow yourself to become more natural. Let your hair get messy and don't comb it for a few days. Stop going to the gym for a while and instead try some natural activities like hiking, chopping wood, or working in a garden. Get back to what's real. Bodies which receive too much specialized attention are like hothouse flowers. They look great as long as they're in the greenhouse receiving all that special fertilizer in a controlled climate, but put them out into the real, everyday world and they quickly fall apart.

Dare to Be Beautiful!

It doesn't matter if you're young or old, a man, woman or an artichoke—dare to be beautiful! Here's the beauty secret of all time: We're all beautiful! Every last one of us. Especially when we are anchored in the One Heart. There's an amazing radiance which just shines through and is stunningly beautiful. I've seen this time and again, during every talk and workshop I've given over the past ten years. Once we step into Oneness there's an astounding transformation that takes place. Everyone, and I mean *everyone*, becomes beautiful! So what, if we have wrinkles or what are judged as physical imperfections by our present social criteria; none of that matters anymore. There's a Light emanating from us which is undeniably gorgeous. It's the greatest beauty secret we have.

Go ahead and dare to be beautiful. Walk out on the streets and let your beauty shine. You know what will happen, don't you? Others will increasingly see your beauty. They will be drawn to you by some special quality of spirit which you emanate, by the power of your Love. Like moths to a candle flame. It's easy, and you don't have to spend hours fixing your hair or makeup or get cosmetic surgery. Simply radiate the Love of the One Heart and dare to show your glowing Core Self.

• Clothing Your Self •

After we've made friends with our body and come to the realization that we're all beautiful, it's time to put on some clothes. What are you going to wear? Please, don't just mindlessly throw on the nearest garments. It's time to stop hiding under our clothing and to reveal our True Selves. Remember, we're here to demonstrate Living Large in all aspects of our life, including clothing. There is great mastery involved in choosing appropriate clothes.

Going into the Closet:
The first step is to go through our closets and see what's really there. As we explore the hidden depths of our closets, we'll discover that we have several different categories of clothing.

Cozy Clothing:
Makes us feel comfortable and cozy, like that old faded flannel shirt and well worn slippers. Keep this stuff because it's always good to have some comforting clothes, especially for those times when our emotional body is feeling delicate or we are tired.

Special Occasion Clothing:
This is clothing for specialized activities such as a ski suit or a ball gown. Look over this stuff carefully and ask yourself, "*Do I still need this?*" Do you really see yourself using flippers soon or wearing that football jacket from High School?

VavaVoom Clothing:
Makes us feel extra gorgeous, fits great and always helps us feel good about ourselves. Keep it and wear it more often!

Next Step Clothing:
Clothing that stretches our being and often represents our future Selves. These we rarely wear because it requires that we are extremely balanced and confidant. But whenever we do wear them, we are taken to a new level. These are very important garments. If you're not yet ready to wear

them out in public, at least try them on at home on a regular basis until you get comfortable with them. If you don't yet have any Next Step Clothes, go shopping and find some. It's a good practice to get more in touch with the new energies you are moving into.

New Normal Clothing:
Everyday clothing which makes you feel good. They fit well and the colors and styles resonate with you. This is because they are in alignment with your Core Self. These are the garments which you're going to wear most of the time.

Sacred Clothing:
Many people don't yet consciously have this type of clothing, and it's important that you do. These are clothes, often in pure white, which are only used for spiritual work such as ceremonies, planetary activations, Sacred Dances. If you have some special clothes set aside for these activities, they will retain the purity of their energies. Each time you put them on, they will raise your vibratory frequencies. It's also an acknowledgment of the high esteem that you give your spiritual activities.

Sacred Clothing doesn't mean that we need to weight ourselves down with heavy ceremonial robes & power medallions. That's old template stuff. Keep it pure and simple!

After sorting out all the previous categories of clothing, take a good, penetrating look at the clothes which remain.

3D Disguises:
These are everything else in our closets. They are our Third Dimensional Disguises and we don't need to clutter our lives with them anymore. So let's get rid of all the clothes which no longer resonate with who we are. Carefully prune

through them and be somewhat ruthless. This includes all the clothing we've acquired which sticks us into a certain role or limited definition. The stuff that we wear because it's there, but doesn't make our hearts sing. Pass it on!

Now, let's find out what our Core Self wants to wear. Let's be real. It's important that all aspects of our being reflect who we really are, and that definitely includes our clothes because clothing is an important part of how we present our Core Self to the world. It also reflects how we feel about ourselves.

We can begin by discovering what clothing our Core Self is aligned with. What types of clothes make you feel comfortable? What colors are you drawn to? Take a deep look at your wardrobe and see where the imbalances are. You may need to acquire some new clothing to rebalance your being. *Some examples:*

Too Cold & Impersonal:

Are most of your clothes of the slick, sophisticated professional category? Are they sending out the message, *"I am not a real person."* If so, perhaps you are losing touch with the simplicity of nature. For balance, try simple, cotton clothing, taking off your sunglasses and going barefoot.

Dressing for Abundance:

If you're having trouble mastering the money/abundance issues so rampant on this planet or if you are trying to establish a new, more successful job, then you might change your style. Start dressing in a less casual & slovenly, more businesslike manner—clean, crisp and together. This is also helpful if you wish to be more efficient. But don't dress to fill a role or you'll be assuming another 3D Disguise; you just want to present a more grounded and alert appearance.

Clothes for Clarity:

If you need increased clarity, check out the way you dress. Are you always sloppy? Are your clothes dirty and rumpled? Are you somewhat disheveled, looking like you just got out of bed? If so, pay some attention to spiffing up your wardrobe and your appearance. You'll soon notice a dramatic change.

Caring for our Clothing:

Here's another area in which we could be much more conscious. Do you continually throw your clothes on the floor in a heap? Do you keep them clean? Do you leave your clothes turned inside out? If you do, it's time to be more aware. For example, if your clothes are inside out, what do you think this does with your energy? It goes inside out.

Another small thing to look at is the alignment of your shoes. Keep them together side-by-side facing the same direction and you will experience greater clarity in your actions. Clothing is an outer reflection of what's inside. Treat them like you would your body and they will serve you exceedingly well.

• Mastering Color •

Colors are an extremely useful tool for healing, recalibration and transformation. Each color has its own keynote and harmonic resonance. Each color is an initiation into wholeness. Within each color there is a wide variety of frequencies, from dense to highly calibrated. Learn to discern the different frequencies of each color and whenever possible, choose the most highly calibrated hues. It's also important to develop an enhanced understanding of the function of color in our daily lives. We can begin by getting to know our personal affinity to individual colors.

Our Home Color:

This is the color that we feel most comfortable with. Cozy, soothing and easy to be with, but not exactly exciting. Many people have the Home Colors of blue or green. It's the color of our starting point and the color that we can always retreat back into in times of distress or imbalance. It's always good to have your Home Color represented in your clothing and home environment.

Our Aspiration Color:

This is the color that we are moving towards. It represents our future and our next step. It's not a color that we wear a lot since we have to be very aligned before we can put it on. But again, it should be represented in both our clothing and home environment. Since we are living in such accelerated times, you might discover that your Aspiration Color changes once you reach your desired level of consciousness. This could happen a few times within your life. Be alert for this change and then make the necessary adjustments.

Our Journey Colors:

The colors that we use to travel from our Home Color to our Aspiration Color. These colors are extremely important because they symbolize our method of propulsion and represent our current initiatory process. Our Journey Color will change many times throughout our lives. Each time it changes, it indicates that we have begun a new phase in our journey. Whenever we start a new phase, we will develop a craving for a new color. At this point, we should seek out this new color and bring it into our surroundings where it can feed our being. Our current Journey Color should be the one which we wear the most. Sometimes, we will have more than one Journey Color at the same time, signifying the multi-layered complexity of what we are experiencing.

Spiraling Through the Full Spectrum:

Ultimately, we need to make friends with all the colors. It is part of becoming a whole being. Search back through your lifetime and make a list of all the colors you have known and loved. Now find the colors which you've never had an affinity with and be on the lookout for opportunities to embrace them.

A special note on the color black:

Black is an unique color which contains all colors and represents the Void. It is especially popular these days in big cities and among young people. In places of heavy energy, black imparts a certain protection to the wearer by covering up vulnerability with a layer of toughness. It also neutralizes your energy and helps you to feel Invisible. Another quality of black is that it absorbs light and radiation. The survivors of the atomic bombs in Japan who wore white fared much better than those wearing black. It makes me wonder about how the holes in the ozone affect those who wear predominantly black clothing.

This planet and all of us living here are in urgent need of increased Light. Because of this, whenever I go to large cities I tend to wear white or bright, cheery colors. This has an amazing effect. It actually spreads the Light and brings positive energy to everyone I encounter. If we want to Live Large and be Beacons of Light, then perhaps, we should be extremely conscious about wearing excessive black during these challenging, final days of duality. There's quite a difference between wearing it because we are really called to do so, and wearing it to be stylish. If you've been wearing black to hide your feelings of vulnerability, maybe it's now time to become comfortable with your vulnerability and show your Core Self.

• Maintaining your Presence in the World •

Wearing the right clothing can really aid us in staying aligned in the Beam while we are out in the world. If you choose clothing which resonates with your Core Self, it will be easier to remain balanced and true to yourself. It is part of our alignment between the inner and outer. Each day check out the condition of the surf, dress to express who you are, do the GO, and you are ready to meet the world from a place of openness, honesty and balance.

• Repatterning our Established Habits •

Most of us don't realize how many ingrained habits we have assumed in our lives. Take a good look at your most mundane everyday activities, all those little things that you do each day in your robot-mode of automatic pilot. Have you noticed that each time you brush your teeth that you do it in exactly the same order? Watch how you wash yourself in the shower. It's always the same regimen. After years of doing the same thing in the same way, these patterns get lodged in our cells and affect our entire being. They also help calcify physical imbalances. I know there's a certain comfort in repetition, but there is also a staleness. It's much easier to remain conscious if we're not operating in our robot-mode. And we are here to become ever more alert and Vibrantly Alive.

So dear ones, let's wake up and be aware of everything we do. Start changing your patterns. When you reach for that bar of soap, try washing in a different order. Shuffle around the ways you do the small things in life. Change those established patterns. Set yourself free!

• Recalibrating our Inner Control Panels •

After we've changed our daily habits, it's time to go deep inside, right to our Inner Control Panels. Go in there and check out the settings. Change anything that isn't where you want it to be. Switch from duality to Oneness, from fear to courage, from lack to abundance, from unworthiness to Love. Look carefully at each setting and choose appropriately. These are important conscious choices we can make for ourselves. Now we are ready to LIVE LARGE!

The secret to

happiness,
liberation
and fulfillment

is to
LIVE LARGE

wherever we are.

THE TWENTY-THIRD KEY:

Living Large Outside

Living Large Outside. . .

Becoming Natural in the World of Nature:

If we want to be fully alive, we need to spend time out in nature. It's easier to be real when we immerse ourselves in the organic life of the natural world. Once we remove ourselves from the fragmented world of man-made distractions, we can move into a more simple, enduring state of being. By reconnecting ourselves to the cycles of nature, we regain our place in the larger cycle. This reconnection with the natural world is something that we unconsciously yearn for and it's an important part of stepping into our wholeness.

Nature is a powerful classroom where there is much to learn. If we are quiet and hone our abilities of observation, we will discover that there are profound discoveries all around us. Learn to listen; sit quietly and watch what is silently revealed. Allow nature to speak to you. There are numerous revelations here. Messages and omens abound. Watch the clouds and see what they are showing you, learn to follow the beckoning of a leaf, listen to the wind in the trees and you will hear the voices of the ancient ones. You will find maps to the cosmos encoded in the rocks, the histories of fallen universes in the grains of sand on a beach. It is all here, just waiting for you to notice it.

• Make Friends With Your Feet •

Let's begin by taking off our shoes. Just forget about shoes for awhile and get to know your virgin feet. Bare feet are natural; we weren't born wearing shoes. Feet are practical tools and wonderful allies. They can take us anywhere. Get to know your feet. Learn to honor them and they will serve you wondrously. Some of us have been friends with our feet all our lives. Our feet are strong and tough, great instruments which take us wherever we need to go. These feet don't need shoes except for when we are walking about in town, in cold weather, or as a fashion statement. If you already have good, well used, practical feet, then all you need do is to keep on loving them, and don't forget to give them some lotion and occasional foot massages.

But if your feet are virtual strangers to you, if you keep them constantly imprisoned in shoes, then there's work to be done. Are your feet all silky and unused like a Chinese concubine's? Would it practically kill you to walk barefoot on the beach? How about a gravel path? Tromping through a forest? Well, there's many people like you on the Earth today. It's amazing, but we've forgotten how to use our natural feet! Our wondrous, natural feet friends!

I've always thought that the easiest way to end war on this planet would be to remove everyone's shoes. So many people would be unable to walk on their naked, natural feet, that war would be impossible. All we would hear would be a bunch of soldiers hobbling about exclaiming, "Ouch!, ouch!, ouch!"

If you're one of the Ouchers, then please take off your shoes and start breaking in your good, old feet. Stop encasing them in heavy shoes where they can't even breathe.

Men are the worst offenders in this category. Big, strong men who can't take five steps without shoes, whose idea of going barefoot is to keep their socks on!

Please, take off your shoes, *and socks*, go outside and feel the Earth through your real feet. Feel that marvelous Sacred Union which takes place between you and the ground. Start out on something soft, like grass, and slowly get them used to being free. After much practice, you'll be able to walk on sharp rocks, even cactus, and your feet will be so beautifully tough that it won't hurt at all. You'll have real, alive, liberated feet!

• Developing Respect for All Life •

Now watch yourself and see how deeply you demonstrate conscious living in every moment. Do you have respect for all life? Observe yourself and see if you are trampling on flowers or scaring away the animals with your loudness. When you stop to pick up a rock, do you just toss it back down or do you replace it lovingly? What do you do with your discarded cigarettes or candy wrappers? Be extremely conscious of every step you take. Walk through nature with a light step, with eyes and heart open—awake, alert and Vibrantly Alive.

Remember to keep on looking at everything with new eyes. For example, what's your attitude to rain? Do you try to avoid getting wet? When it rains, do you react with unconscious, ingrained responses such as, *"Oh no, it's raining!"*, treating rain as if it were something bad. Think about it for a minute. Rain is a blessing. It gives nourishment to all of life. It's lush with those wonderful negative ions which we all need and it washes everything clean. Why are we so happy to get wet when we go swimming and so distressed to get wet when it rains? Love the rain. Don't be afraid to get wet, just go out and let it wash over you. Think of it as a gigantic waterfall coming from the heavens. A bounteous waterfall of Love.

Here's something else you can incorporate into your life. Each time that you encounter a natural source of water, you should greet it properly. This includes oceans, lakes, springs, rivers, waterfalls, natural pools and streams. Sit down beside the water and speak to it in Star Language. Tell it who you are and that you are here in honor and Love. Then following the Splash Technique mentioned in the previous chapter, wash yourself in the water. I always add a few extra touches by tossing some water on the top of my head and finish my ritual by scooping up the water in my hands and holding it up to the sky.

• Weather Patterns Mirror the Prevailing Energies •

Each weather pattern has a purpose. It reflects the prevailing energy currents and will tell you much about the condition of the Surf. Learn to align yourself with the weather. Blend your activities with the prevailing patterns. Constantly refine your perceptions until you can read the many different types of wind, the myriad snowfalls and adjust your activities accordingly so you can work with the inherent energies, rather than against them.

Learn to listen to the winds and you will receive messages. Watch the shifting patterns of the clouds and see visions. The weather patterns contain numerous maps and clues to the Greater Reality. This refinement of knowledge of the weather is still practiced by some indigenous people. The

Inuits have over twenty-five words to describe different types of snow and the Polynesians have an extensive vocabulary delineating various aspects of the ocean.

Here are some examples of wind to get you started:

• Winds of Change •

A strong, searing wind which blows away the old and brings in the New. This wind should be welcomed. Go outside and let it strip your old layers off. Hold nothing back and surrender to the glorious Winds of Change. Your Core Self will exult in this wind. Winds of Change are pregnant with the New. Open yourself to them and you will feel the seeds of your future imbedding within you.

• Stripping Wind •

A wind which strips away the old and purifies the world. It is cold, penetrating and somewhat raw. Stay indoors while it cleanses the outside.

• Winds of Love •

A gentle, yet penetrating wind which brings Love to you. Often found on those deliciously perfect Spring days. This breezy wind will lightly dance on your face, playfully loving you. Love is in the air!

• Mean Winds •

They are heavy and thick, full of powerful gusts which blow away any loose objects. Outdoor furniture goes flying, shingles come off your roof. Mean Winds howl and shriek. There is a sense of foreboding connected to this wind. It feels as if something ominous and mysterious is happening. It's a good time to stay indoors. Mean Winds aren't really mean; they are just telling us that the natural world needs to reassert and recalibrate itself. That it's time for humans to be quiet and let nature predominate. Out in nature, the Wild Things come out to dance. This is their time to celebrate. The balance is restored between the natural world and the man-made world.

• Winds of Approval •

This is a wind which comes to you in confirmation of your alignment with the Beam. Sometimes, you will experience this when you arrive at a sacred site. It signifies approval of your presence there. Often there will be Winds of Approval when we are making a sacred ceremony. They can be short gusts of strong wind that suddenly appear and quickly die away or repeated puffs of billowing wind. Usually, Winds of Approval arrive unexpectedly on a windless day. Listen to them and move into a deeper Oneness.

• Winds of the Ancient Ones •

This is the wind through the trees in a forest. Listen carefully and you will hear the ancient voices of our ancestors whispering to you. Speak to them in Star Language and they will tell you whatever you need to know. This sacred wind is especially powerful in old growth forests with the ancient tree beings.

• Winds in the Bamboo •

Bamboo forests are magical places. When wind passes through a bamboo grove it makes the sound of heaven. A doorway to other worlds opens. . .

• Dragon Wind •

An extremely rare wind which is caused by dragons circling in the sky. As they churn up the air, powerful currents are stirred; massive changes are set in motion. The nature kingdom wakes up and the fairies begin to sing. Listen to their songs and sing along with your whole heart. Nothing will ever be the same. It is a great blessing to experience a Dragon Wind.

It is also said that a huge Dragon Wind will sweep over the Earth when the Doorway of the 11:11 closes at the end of 2011, blowing away the final traces of duality.

• Dancing the Dance of Creation •

Practice walking as a Divine Being. Act as if you were the Co-Creator of this entire world and all of nature are your beloved kin. Speak to your kin in Star Language; sing to them. Treat everything and everyone with deep Love and respect. That little ant is part of your beloved family, that shell, bird and plant. See the sky, the ocean, the mountains, the lakes, streams, trees and stars, as your brothers and sisters and greet them with Love. See them as equals with you, all Divine Beings participating in the Dance of Creation.

When you are able to do this, something miraculous happens. There's a subtle shift into a heightened reality. Here, you can receive wondrous revelations, you can sing the Song of One. We all share the same core of Essence. We are united in the One Heart and form One Vast Being. A profound sense of peaceful well-being will embrace you. It is the totality of the One.

THE TWENTY-FOURTH KEY:

Mastering Service

Mastering Service. . .

"To rule truly is to serve.". . . I Ching

One of the greatest ways we can fulfill ourselves in this lifetime is to Master the Art of Service. True serving gives us magnificent, unprecedented opportunities to utilize our full beings; it stretches us beyond our previous boundaries. When we become Master Servers, we enter into a state of heightened awareness. Our entire being is engaged in the act of service, and we are able to express our full capabilities. We become Vibrantly Alive.

By serving ourselves, we serve others.
By serving others, we serve ourselves.

True Service entails a widened perspective, a deeply anchored sense of Oneness. When we are consciously woven into Oneness, we know that we are all part of a vaster One Being. Whenever we serve our One Being in any capacity, large or small, we are also serving ourselves. There is no more sense of separation between the individual beings within the One. Aligned with the One Being, we feel all aspects of the One. We are part of the collective wholeness of our One. If any part of our greater One Being is feeling anguish or exhilaration, lack of love or bounteous joy, it is felt by all. We not only access these emotions, but we can also be affected by them.

*There is no more separation
between here and there,
between ourself and others.*

This is one of the bedrock foundations of Living Large. This is why we are called upon to serve as never before. True Service is not slavery or being a doormat for others to walk upon. It is not being used or abused. In the Template of Oneness there are no more *givers* and *takers*. We all give our finest and receive the finest.

Service is our joyful expression of Love for our One Being. It is a natural part of who we are. We are in service, not because we *have to* or *should*, but because it is our delight and fulfillment to serve. Service utilizes our full being and makes us feel more alert and alive. It is extremely empowering and gives us continual opportunities to access our Core Selves and openly manifest our inherent magnificence. By allowing ourselves to become Master Servers, we transcend much of our duality-based personalities and step into new, previously unaccessed, heightened levels of ourselves. We have finally become Vibrantly Alive, naturally responsive, mature, liberated True Beings.

How do we become Master Servers?

The first step is to continually look beyond yourself. LOOK LARGER. You can begin from that old vantage point of standing high above the Earth and looking down upon it. Carefully observe what's going on down there. What needs to be done? How can you participate? How can you help? Embrace the planet and all its life-forms in the Love of the One Heart. Just hold it and love everything. Keep part of your being in this vantage point at all times.

Now step back into your life and look around you. What needs to be done? How can you help? This is where empowerment comes in. If you see a need, do it. Don't wait around until you are asked to help. Remain aware at all times of what is going on around you. And please remember that this isn't a mental process; it's a *feeling* of the energies surrounding you. You can feel them because they are part of your Vaster Being.

Opportunities for True Service abound. They are ever present. Learn to see them and when you do, act upon it unhesitatingly. You can serve simply by maintaining a positive outlook, or by washing dishes that are dirty, even if you're not the one responsible for them. Serve by sharing your Love with everyone you encounter; serve by cleaning up your own messes. Serve by becoming aware of your own needs as well as the needs of others.

Master Servers don't only serve when they feel like it, or when optimum conditions are present. They serve whenever the need is there. Often, this translates as being on call twenty-four hours a day. But remember that these opportunities for service are gifts—glorious opportunities to step beyond our smaller selves and manifest our true magnificence.

THE TWENTY-FIFTH KEY:

The Power of the Journey

The Power of the Journey. . .

We are presently undergoing an incredible journey into the Unknown.

It is an unprecedented journey which will take us into realms previously unexplored or imagined. We have crossed the threshold of the final frontier which leads to totally new levels of consciousness and heightened states of being. And although we might be scattered all across the planet, we are making this journey together.

It is a journey full of greatness which requires our total commitment, focused intent, wholehearted Love and courage. We must always be ready to shift perspectives, to rearrange our belief systems and to surrender all that we have achieved so far. This entails a continual process of renewal, being careful not to get stuck or calcified in any specific phase of our greater journey. Each day we are being reborn into an ever vaster reality. We must remain fluid and open, always aligned with the subtle currents of the Invisible. And embrace the pregnant emptiness of the Unknown.

Our Core Selves will lead the way; all we have to do is to follow, to dare to finally become fully alive. To learn to Love with our total beings. TO BE THE LOVE. We are on a journey of resurrection, transcendence and rebirth. We are becoming illuminated with the iridescence of the heightened frequencies of the INVISIBLE. The Seed Core of our cells is being transfigured with illumination. All of our various energy bodies are coming into alignment in One Vaster Being—the physical, emotional, mental & spiritual bodies as well as our core Earth & Star Selves. More of our fragmentary selves are unifying into One Being than ever before.

This magnificent journey into the Unknown sweeps us along a path of many windings. It's so easy to become impatient with all the time it's taking, with all the steps we have to make. We want to reach our destination NOW; we want to immerse ourselves in the New. We want to live in a New World—a world that finally has meaning—that is filled with Love and Truth. We want to create Islands of Light, and experience fulfilling love relationships. We want to be able to openly express our True Selves. And why is it taking so long? Why do we have to pass through so much illusion? Why is the journey so arduous and never-ending?

The Power is in the Journey.

That's right; *the power is in the journey.* Not the long sought after destination, but the journey itself. The process of our journey gives us exactly what we need to birth our True Selves. It constantly recalibrates our beings and sets us free from the limitations of duality. The journey is the receptacle for our initiatory process. By undergoing this journey, we are creating the New World. It is being created within our very beings, in the transfigured cells of our physical bodies, and within the world outside. We are the midwives of this rebirth. The journey itself is our birth canal, leading us from duality to Oneness. And as with any birth, a large part of ourselves and our previous reality systems must die in order to be reborn. This is why our journey is often arduous and challenging. Why we must live in a constant state of surrender and openness. Why we must make our commitment to go the distance with everything we've got.

Once we have done that, we can surrender our destination. Letting go of any of our imagined outcomes or goals. None of them are accurate anyway, since our real destination is *far beyond* our present levels of perception.

Stand right where you are in this very moment and accept your journey. Embrace all the needed experiences it brings to you. Everything is absolutely perfect. Your journey is the perfect setup which is personally designed with finely calibrated precision to help you birth your True Self and step into the deeper Invisible. Anything you need to work on or recalibrate will be brought to you and magnified to get your full attention, whether you like it or not!

Journeying through the Invisible into utterly new realms of consciousness is always challenging, but never more so than now. The deeper we go, the less of our old tools, maps, abilities, knowledge & attainments can be used. We have to be guided by our hearts, our finely honed intuition, our surfing skills and by unvarnished truth. This has to be at a core level—real, raw, stripped of illusion. Fortunately, we are presently being given all the experiences we need to get us pared down to this core level. So the next time you find yourselves in the depths of despair, or numbed by the unreality and lifelessness of existence, please remember that this is part of the process of being stripped down to your core. We need to do this before we can complete our birth. *It is the power of the journey in action.*

Take a good, deep look at where you are right now. This is your current transit point upon your journey. Look around you; scan your life and your surroundings with renewed clarity. They are full of the key elements which will take you to your next step. What needs to be done? What needs to be recalibrated? What do you need to release? Lessons and evolutionary triggers abound, if you only take the time to see them.

We are always in a state of transit;
We are always in the eternal Now.

The eternal Now contains everything—past, present, future rolled up into a big sphere that expands into all-encompassing vastness. Simultaneously, we are all in a state of transit, traveling upon our great journey into the deeper Unknown. Because of this transitory nature of shifting realities, everything here on Earth is temporary. It is all just flickering plays of energy, ever dancing frequencies of Light.

If you can see this, then perhaps, you will understand how totally futile it is to try to hold onto outward form. How useless are our puny attempts at asserting control or imposing limitations upon the limitless. If we walk through life with our hearts and hands wide open, not trying to hold onto anything, we will keep on growing and transforming. We will keep ourselves receptive to continual renewal and rebirth. We will quicken our beings with true aliveness. Thus will we honor the power of the journey.

THE TWENTY-SIXTH KEY:

The Remnant Seed

The Remnant Seed. . .

Remnant Seed:
The physical sign, trace or vestige
    of something which no longer exists.

The Remnant Seed were here at the beginning. They existed even before the beginning and aided in the creation of this planet. They carry within them the patterning of all things, the universal key to creation. Also encoded within their cells are the seeds of the Greater Reality. They are the Keepers of the Matrix.

Think of a supernova, still physically visible to us now, yet something which burned itself out long ago. Dinosaur bones which carry the DNA of a species which no longer exists. Ancient people like the Hopi, Dogon, Bön or Kalahari Bushmen who served as the anchor points for the establishment of this present world which is now in its final days. There are the Australian Aboriginals, the most ancient people still living on this planet, who have held together our star maps for countless thousands of years. And there's the great, ancient tree beings, gentle giants living in our rapidly diminishing old growth forests who are being decimated and cut down daily by ignorant people motivated solely by greed. The whales with their vast storehouses of knowledge who grace this planet's oceans.

The vestige of something which no longer exists.

We, the awakened ones, are also the Remnant Seed. The ones who remember. Within our cellular memory banks are the histories of all known worlds, myriad worlds yet unborn, as well as those far beyond our present level of understanding. All this is carried within the Seed Core of our beings.

We hold the memories of ancient times far beyond the most expanded reach of recorded history. We remember when Angels walked openly upon this planet, the time when giants ruled, the flourishing Fairy Kingdoms. We have sung the song of the stars; we have flown through the skies on wings of light; we have swam through the oceans as whales and dolphins. We have watched numerous continents rise and fall each time the Earth shifts its axis. We have experienced the birth and death of stars, the transformation of galaxies. We have loved with bodies of flesh, fur, feathers, music, pure geometry and light.

Encoded within us is the radiating sphere of ALL-TIME—No-Time, No-Space. We contain the *Past That Never Was*, the *Future Which Never Will Be*, and the *Present Which Is Far More Than It Seems*. Each of us is a perfect hologram of the One.

Something which no longer exists. . .

We are the Remnant Seed. Our physical bodies are the vestiges of something which no longer exists. They were formed as the Template of our Creator, or maps of God, in the old evolutionary spiral we are currently transcending. Our bodies were established as the central focus, or homebase, for our passage through duality, so we could maintain a sense of separate identity. Our physical forms defined our known parameters. They kept us anchored into the physical world and strengthened our acceptance of a duality-based belief system as our predominant reality.

Our true vastness was the Great Mystery that was kept hidden from us. Our spiritual awareness was limited to what could be discovered and attained within the Spirituality of Duality. Our goal was defined as enlightenment and liberation. What remained a secret until recently was that enlightenment and liberation are our natural state of being. We already are that.

Our journey of reawakening brought us a remembrance of our inherent vastness. This journey took us to the very portals of Oneness. It enabled us to quantum leap into the uncharted realms of the Invisible. Here, we finally merge our full vastness into the physical.

This creates a new, *heightened physical* which can no longer be encased within previous definitions of limitation, separation or matter. The concept of our bodies as the maps of God is now obsolete, for it is much greater than that. This new, Vibrantly Alive physical has been quickened with the vibratory resonance of Oneness. The Stars have embedded into the Earth. The calcification of duality has dissolved. Everything is totally different than before. The physical has been reconfigured to encompass the vastness of the One.

Many people ask if we will still have physical bodies in the Template of Oneness? We probably will, but they will be nothing like our old ones. Perhaps they will look similar, but they will be new, *heightened physical* forms permeated with Light frequencies *which are totally merged with our vastness.* This will make it an absolutely new physical. We are currently in the process of transforming our bodies from the old, limited physical dimension to the new *heightened physical* encompassing Vastness.

Encoded within us are the seeds of the Greater Reality.

While we are the vestige of something which no longer exists, we also contain the seeds of the Greater Reality. Encoded within our cells is the New Matrix, the map of the world which is being born. These seeds of the New Matrix provide our real nourishment as we increasingly release our attachment to the realms of duality. They are the beacon which propels us forward into ever deeper sectors of the Invisible.

The Remnant Seed are Keepers of the Matrix.

We stand at the centerpoint of a double helix spiral. One spiral is the old matrix; the other is the matrix of the Greater Reality. We stand in the center of the sphere of NOW. We hold the matrix for past, present & future. From this position the New can be born.

THE TWENTY-SEVENTH KEY:

The Lovers from Beyond the Stars

The Lovers from Beyond the Stars. . .

Far beyond the most distant stars. . .

One Vast Being—expanding far beyond the most distant stars. Holding all the worlds within worlds within its tender embrace. One Vast Being—so stretched out that it appears to be two. Each half of this One Being is positioned at opposite ends of the known universe. They are known as the Lovers from Beyond the Stars.

The Lovers from Beyond the Stars call out to one another with their deepest longing. This yearning to consciously merge back into One Being is the core essence of our own yearning for true Sacred Union. Through their focused intent they hold the worlds within worlds in positional alignment. The purity of their Love quickens the Spaces-in-Between, bridging the gap between spirals that every fragment of ourselves may experience the fulfillment of perfect union and Oneness.

The Lovers from Beyond the Stars hold the Template for the Greater Love. *They are the Template.* They represent the highest level of Ecstatic Love which can be experienced within the transitional zone of the 11:11. They are the entry point to the Greater Love. This entry point is created once the Lovers from Beyond the Stars reunite back into One Being.

All the great, legendary lovers throughout the ages have been personifications of the Lovers from Beyond the Stars. By rising into conscious embodiment of the Lovers from Beyond the Stars, we bring to completion the ancient love stories. These stories are fulfilled as all the legendary lovers are finally reunited. They now merge into One Being. We move beyond their personified stories into the purer core resonance of the essence beyond, that of the Lovers from Beyond the Stars.

We are the Lovers from Beyond the Stars...

Here's how to embody the Lovers from Beyond the Stars. You can do this by yourself or with another person. If you choose to do it with a partner, then pick someone with whom you are deeply aligned. You both must be prepared to open yourselves up wider than ever before. Be wild, be raw, be free and don't worry if you're going to look or act weird. If you're really experiencing the energy, you *will* look and act rather strange, for you'll be embodying a very unworldly essence. You will discover that your body movements will become slower and more stylized, expressing a natural elegance. When you make your calls to your Lover from Beyond the Stars, let your heart's core be expressed. This is not a time to be polite or worry about what kind of impression you are making. Be real and express your Core Self.

Begin by opening your mouth and breathing as if you were blowing. Keep your lips in this extended position and breath through your open mouth throughout this process.

To get in touch with this vast part of yourself, you must first position yourself at the far edge of the known universe, far beyond the most distant star. Sit there quietly and see yourself as one half of a much greater being. Feel your deep yearning for Sacred Union with that other part of yourself. Let this yearning flood your being. *Embody the yearning.*

Directly in front of you are the myriad dimensional universes—worlds within worlds—spinning, spiraling. Go beyond these worlds, stretching your awareness to the far reaches of the known universe. There, beyond the most distant star, is the other half of your One Being—your Lover from Beyond the Stars. Feel its presence begin to stir as it senses you. Feel its deep longing to reunite with you back into One Being. Feel the immense power and precious purity of your Love. Feel the focused intent which eternally binds you together. See how small the dimensional universes have become. They are simply small spinning specks of dust flying through the waves of your longing.

Using Star Language, call out to your Lover from Beyond the Stars. Call out from the heart of your Core Self. Let your cries be filled with waves of Love, with your deepest longing to reunite with your most precious beloved. Call out what you have never dared express before. Send your heart's call across the vast expanse of worlds within worlds—far beyond the most distant star. Feel the resonance of your Love traveling through the Spaces-in-Between.

After you have sent forth your call, sit quietly and listen carefully. . . Soon, you will hear the answering call from your Lover from Beyond the Stars. . . Let these vibrations of Ecstatic Love fill your being. Drink them deeply; let them melt into your cells; feel embraced by them. . . Now reply with your full being, with the vast, untapped reservoir of your Love. Make your calls together, letting them simultaneously overlap one another until an entirely new resonance is birthed. This new resonance of conscious union serves to quicken the Spaces-in-Between, heightening the energy of Ecstatic Love, aligning all the worlds within worlds into the One Heart.

Feel yourself as One Vast Being. As you step into a greater vastness within your Core Self you will transcend all sense of limitation and separation. The distance between you will shrink into nothingness as full, perfect Sacred Union will be achieved. You have reached the entry point into the Greater Love. There is an open portal here. When it reveals itself, you may step through and go where no-one has gone before, into the purest realms of the Greater Love. This is the apex of the Second Gate Initiation and the starting point for all future endeavours.

Once this open portal into the Greater Love is entered, the Template of True Love is turned inside out and the Lovers from Beyond the Stars cease to be. Instead, there is an enlarged map of the Greater Love to explore.

Our Bodies are Maps of the Lovers from Beyond the Stars.

Our physical bodies are perfect maps of the Lovers from Beyond the Stars and the One Being that they form. Our hands represent the Lovers from Beyond the Stars. You can place one hand at the side of your head with the palm facing forwards. This represents you as Lover. Now stretch your other hand as far in front of you as possible with your palm turned towards you. This hand represents your Lover. Feel the worlds within worlds between you. Feel the purity of your Love, the deep yearning to reunite; feel your focused intent.

Now very slowly, move your hands to a position where your elbows extend out to your sides, your forearms go straight up into the air and your palms are facing each other on either side of our head. As you make this movement, I want you to feel the shift as you move from a Lover from Beyond the Stars into alignment with your other half, then unite into One Vaster Being. When you become One Being, you will reside within your entire body.

Stand up and take a few steps with your One Being. Feel how much vaster and more alive you become when you do this. It shifts your entire being onto a new map. We are creating the foundation for our New Selves in our new lives. Try to stay in this new level of awareness as much as possible. Keep doing this practice until you continually embody the One Being.

This transformation into One Being is extremely profound. It marks the time when two previously separate beings become One. They do this by each taking the next direct step on their individual evolutionary paths. Their next steps lead them into this deep level of Sacred Union. Their personal evolutionary paths blend into one. Although they still have two physical bodies, they have aligned on a cellular level into One Being.

This is the key of the Second Gate Initiations. Sacred Union will be greatly enhanced when we enter the Third Gate in 1997 and move into a much larger expansion of our Oneness.

THE TWENTY-EIGHTH KEY:

As the Spiral Turns

As the Spiral Turns. . .

Seeing the Big Picture.

Stop for a moment if you will, and see where you are. Let's look at the larger picture and get our bearings. There's a rather unique situation happening here on planet Earth during these momentous times.

We are in the midst of the Time of Completion which means that it's the final days of the reign of duality and it's certainly not going to be dull. There are going to be tremendous changes during the next several years, *unprecedented changes;* so we might as well get used to this and learn to go with the flow. It will help if we can accept change gracefully and not try to stubbornly hold onto *the way things used to be.* Because they're never going to be that way again. Much of what we've known and accepted as *normal* is going to disappear from our lives. Again, we might as well accept this as cheerfully as possible, because it's going to happen, whether we want it to or not. Adaptability is a great virtue to develop these days.

We are standing in the center of a double helix spiral. This is the Zone of Overlap between the spiral of duality and that of Oneness. This is a Transitional Zone, signifying that it is a temporary condition; something which only exists for a brief time. This Zone of Overlap is a bridge between two, very different, evolutionary spirals. Which means that there are two simultaneous, overlapping reality systems that we are dealing with each day. No wonder we get confused sometimes! Transitional Zones are always somewhat awkward and uncomfortable. They often challenge us to the very core, but they do take us to a new place.

We are also located within the center of the radiating sphere of No-Time. This sphere contains the *Past That Never Was,* the *Future That Never Will Be,* and the *Present Which Is Far More Than It Seems* merged into the eternal NOW. Time itself has been turned inside out and is in the process of being completely transcended.

We are anchored in the One Heart, the foundation for the Greater Love. This signifies that we are on the threshold of embodying deeper, truer levels of Love than we ever imagined possible. The separation between "I" and "you" is dissolving to reveal an All-Encompassing Oneness. This leads us into consciously becoming One Being. Our Unified Being is so vast that we transcend the boundaries of space. There is no more *here* and *there,* no more distance between us.

Our evolutionary timetable has quantum leaped onto a much more accelerated patterning. Leaps in consciousness that used to take us several lifetimes to achieve can now be made in an instant. We are no longer bound by old timing mechanisms. There is a new timing mechanism in effect called the Timing Chain which is aligned with the Greater Reality. It is in the patterning of the fully activated One Heart. Right now we are approaching a major intersection on the Timing Chain, one that will irrevocably alter the course of our lives.

What goes around, comes around. . .

In our unique stance in the center of the double helix spirals, we are experiencing an unprecedented fusion of two evolutionary spirals. This fusion is taking place in the very core of our beings. We become the melting pot of the old and the New, containing within our beings both completions and new beginnings woven together in Oneness.

Many cycles are being brought to completion; numerous spirals are reaching their appointed conclusions and returning to their points of origin. As this happens, we are being given tremendous opportunities to jump off the old spirals by transcending them and to move on to our next level of evolution *on an entirely new map*. The famous Ouroboros serpent is now swallowing his tail. Soon, his entire body will be consumed and he will be turned inside out. NOW IS THE TIME to make our quantum leaps!

Some examples of spirals which are presently evolving:

• Numbers •

In the Template of Duality we were governed by a set numerical system. This numerical system was based on the numbers One through Nine. Anything beyond that was broken down into the resonance of One through Nine. In the Time of Completion we are floating in the pool of the Nine. Nine is the number of completion and signifies that we have reached the end of the old road. It is the fusion of all numbers, much like black is the fusion of all the colors.

From the center of the pool of the Nine, we can quantum leap onto a new numerical patterning of Master Numbers. Master Numbers are the double digit numbers: 11, 22, 33,

44, 55, 66, 77, 88 & 99. The entry point into this new numerical patterning is the Master Number 11. Eleven announces the entrance of something totally New, much like a lightning bolt and is associated with the planet Uranus. *(Uranus is significant because it is the only planet in our solar system which has a direct link to Beyond the Beyond.)* Eleven is the Messenger of the New & Unexpected and is the core unit of all the Master Numbers.

Next comes the Master Number 22 which is composed of two Elevens (11:11) and is the Master Vibration for building on the New. This number is currently being activated within us. The 33 is also being introduced. It is the Master Number for Universal Service through conscious alignment into Oneness. *(The dates of both the 11:11 and Second Gate Activations each added up to Thirty-Three.)* The rest of the Master Numbers have yet to be introduced because we haven't reached the level of consciousness where they can be activated. But they will be, as soon as we are ready.

Double Master Numbers are extremely powerful triggers to activate encodings within our cellular memory banks. They are insertion points for the Greater Reality to enter. So far, the only one we have experienced is 11:11, but look at what it has achieved!

Once we enter the patterning of Master Numbers, there is no going back into the limited concepts of the One through Nine. A repatterning must take place from our old formats of 3, 7, 9 & 12 into the heightened vibrations of the Master Numbers. *(This is an illustration of why the "12:12" Activation had nothing to do with the 11:11.)* We should start using Master Numbers wherever we can: in our architecture, our ceremonies, and our daily lives. Remember the refrain of the Og-Min, "No-Down, No-Return!"

• Colors •

Our established color spectrum is also undergoing a huge transformation. Our available spectrum is, but a small part of the known color spectrum. Much as there are many sounds which we cannot hear, there are many colors which we cannot yet see. These undiscovered colors emanate from the Invisible. They are composed of heightened vibrancy and are filled with shimmering iridescence.

In order to reach the level of awareness where we can see the extended spectrum, we must first make our journey through the known rainbow. Each color represents a level of initiation, a merger into greater Oneness. If you look at our known rainbow, you will see that the color green is in the center position—the place of the heart. This is why green is such a healing color. Trees, plants, & grass are all green; they heal and nourish us by absorbing our carbon dioxide and giving out oxygen. We could not live in this old world without the color green. Green is aligned with the number Four, the number of the Four Directions and the Four Pillars which hold up the planet.

If you take the arc of our available rainbow and bend it upwards into a circle (or spiral), with green remaining on the bottom, you will see that a new color appears in the upper part of the circle opposite green. This is magenta which is created by the merger of red & purple, the opposite poles of our old rainbow. Magenta represents the marriage of Sun & Moon, the balancing and unification of polarities within our own inner beings. Magenta is aligned with the number 44 *(four Elevens)*, which means that it is our launching pad and entry point into a new evolutionary spiral.

This rainbow circle is the color map of the evolutionary cycle, or spiral, which we are now in the process of transcending. As we do so, magenta will shift from being our capstone to become our new foundation. Some of us have already made the leap into this new evolutionary spiral and are standing on the new foundation of magenta. Our new capstone is iridescent. We have entered the realms of the Invisible.

Just in case you are curious, I will mention a little about the map of the cycle before our current one. In Earth history terms, this would be referred to as the Ante-Diluvian World, the map of the times before the Great Flood. The base color was brown which is the masculine Earth color. At the top of the rainbow circle were blue and yellow which created the capstone of green, the feminine Earth color.

Making our own personal journey through the rainbow, we travel through all the known colors until we reach magenta. After we have merged with the powerful initiations of magenta, we arrive at white. This is an important stage in our journey, for white signifies purity, emptiness, openness and Oneness. We have now entered the Invisible. After we become familiar with the early stages of the Invisible through white, we can return to the other colors. As we do this, we will discover that the colors themselves have shifted and a new heightened vibrancy has appeared.

• Legends •

Many of our old legends were purposely left incomplete. They laid out the story, pointed out the lessons, but never brought things to a conclusion. This is because true resolution could not be achieved within the Template of Duality until we, ourselves, had moved to a new evolutionary level. So we now find ourselves in a most interesting time when our ancient legends are finally being completed. As this happens, we shall be truly liberated from the *Past That Never Was*.

A by-product of this is the dissolving away of ancient prophecies. For they too, were created within the old patterning. As we increasingly anchor our beings in Oneness, the harmonic resonance of the entire planet is shifted, wiping away our old evolutionary timetable. Once this is transformed, old prophecies and predictions will have nothing to base themselves upon. This is how we birth the New and create our very own future.

• Great Loves •

As mentioned in the previous chapter, the cycle of the Great Lovers is coming to a close. All the stories of legendary lovers throughout history such as Isis & Osiris, Tristan & Isolde, Arthur & Guinevere, served to keep alive the flame of True Love. They were simply personifications of the Lovers from Beyond the Stars. Once we embody the Lovers from Beyond the Stars, the legendary lovers fulfill their Higher Purpose. This frees them to unite into One Being and move into the Greater Love.

• Spiritual Beings •

As we leave the realm of duality and anchor our beings in Oneness, we step beyond the realm of personified spiritual beings & established spiritual hierarchies. In the Template of Oneness, there is only the One. There are no more Ascended Masters, Guardian Angels, Archangels, Gods & Goddesses, Ashtar Command, Intergalactic Confederation,

Dark Lords, Lords of Light, Great White Brotherhood, or spirit guides & teachers. We have all moved to a new level of equality—Oneness.

This is a major step of initiation, a great empowerment. It happens naturally when you first anchor yourself into the Invisible. You look around in this vast emptiness, trying to find your way, trying to use your old maps, skills & spiritual practices, and discover that nothing works. That's when you call upon the old great spiritual beings who helped get you here in the Invisible. Silence... That's all you hear... This can, admittedly, be quite disconcerting, for this is exactly the point in which you feel the most vulnerable, lost and alone. Sometimes, a few of our old spiritual role models may appear, but when they do, they are tiny! This is even worse than no response. It makes you feel really stranded in the Invisible.

This feeling of abandonment by the spiritual hierarchies is extremely challenging. It would be easy to give up the journey into the Invisible at this point, but for one small matter. *We can't.* Just try to go back into *the way things used to be,* and you will discover that it's simply impossible. So you might as well get used to this new turn of events. As we increasingly step into our own Mastery, we will become more comfortable in the great Unknown.

The next shocker is that God, him/herself, no longer exists as a personified being. The God that we knew and loved as the Supreme Being in the Template of Duality was simply a personification of the One. While we were anchored in duality, subject to the overriding illusion of separation, we needed to believe in a Supreme Being. So the One helpfully projected a personified fragment of itself to us which we could look up to as God. Now we have entered a much vaster zone of awareness in which nothing is separate from the One. The One is All-Encompassing. We are all part of the One.

If the spiral turns for one of us, it turns for all of us.

We are all journeying together as One. This includes every living being on this planet and the Earth herself. Each time that any one of us makes a breakthrough in consciousness, the spiral turns and everyone moves upwards a notch upon the evolutionary spiral. As we shift spirals from duality to Oneness, this creates a major shifting upon the spiral of duality. The calcification of duality loosens and all beings evolve.

THE TWENTY-NINTH KEY:

The Shattering of All of All Known Worlds

The Shattering of All Known Worlds. .

When the world as we know it shatters,
when we have nowhere to go,
but to the Unknown.

Then we shall be given
something New to stand on,
or we shall be taught how to fly!

There comes a time in our journey into the Invisible when the world as we know it shatters. Everything which we have held dear and sacred is either broken or becomes suddenly irrelevant. The props are removed from our stage and the rug is pulled out from under our feet. Everything is topsy-turvy, upside down, disarranged and broken. Old, trusted friends disappear, important relationships wither or turn strange, and our tried and true spiritual practices become totally ineffective. The bubble of our previous belief system bursts wide open. Welcome to: The Shattering of All Known Worlds.

This is an important stage on our journey into the deeper Invisible. And it's one of the most difficult times we will experience. It will challenge us to our very core. And beyond even that. . . Which is exactly where we need to be.

We will be stripped bare, turned inside out, rearranged, cleansed, and purified anew. This is a tremendously powerful time of purging, a great dying away of the old. Let it happen. Cry, sob, get angry; react however you like, but allow it to happen and persevere.

**Our old worlds must shatter
in order to create the New.**

The Shattering of All Known Worlds breaks our old inner templates. These are the templates which have molded us to established behavior patterns, well worn habits, stale preferences, baseless assumptions and limited boundaries. If you have been deeply entrenched in old patterning, it will often take a pretty powerful shattering to set you free.

Shattering is a death experience and to be effective, it's usually strong. But please remember, that like everything else, it will soon pass and it is serving a purpose. The sooner you can surrender the old, the quicker it will be complete. As the adage goes, *"The bigger the death, the bigger the rebirth!"* Well, we do want a huge rebirth; we want to live in the New as Vibrantly Alive Earth-Star Beings. So please persevere. Let those old worlds come tumbling down.

When the dust finally settles and you are resting quietly amidst the debris of yesterday's reality, then you are finally ready to enter the egg. . .

THE THIRTIETH KEY:

Inside the Egg

A Pregnant Emptiness. . .

Inside the Egg. . .

Floating inside a pregnant egg.

An all-pervading sense of emptiness.

Everything is filled with emptiness. . .

Our old selves have died away and our New Selves wait to be born. We are in the heightened state of active receptivity known as I-Await. We have done the inner work of recalibrating our beings and rewriting our scripts. There is nothing more for us to do. We can't go out seeking our futures, nor can we make any plans. Nothing can be achieved until our New Selves are born.

Feel all the old forms stretching wide open. . .

Now is the time to cut our boats free from the dock.

Let them slowly drift away,
   far out into the distant horizon

until they move naturally into their new positions.

Floating in the egg,

waiting. . .

for the New to be born,

waiting. . .

for our futures to reveal themselves. . .

THE THIRTY-FIRST KEY:

Accepting the Unacceptable

Accepting the Unacceptable. . .

Accepting our present reality, opens the door to change!

We have stripped down to our Core Selves. We have recalibrated our inner beings, cleared out the clutter—become so much more real. By doing this we have rewritten our inner scripts. Our New Selves are finally in the process of being born. So much has changed, and we are truly not the same people we used to be. There's only one slight problem. We are becoming New, but our outer reality is still the same. It no longer reflects our New Selves. What to do?

Our next step is to Accept the Unacceptable. First, take a good look around you and see where you are. Then get in touch with your heart and feel where you really want to be. How could your outer reality change to more perfectly reflect your True Self? What does your heart want to do? Be still and feel the deepest calling of your heart. When you can feel this clearly, don't start running around and making plans. Don't try to make anything happen. Just feel what you really want in your life so your outer reality can be aligned with your new inner Self.

Now, take another good look around you and Accept the Unacceptable. This means that we are going to accept every element present in our lives at this very moment. This is what we're given to work with RIGHT HERE, RIGHT NOW. Accept that this is what you've created in your life up until now. Please remember that accepting is not the same as resigning yourself or making compromises. *We don't have to do that anymore!* Hopefully, we stopped doing that a long time ago. We're simply going to gently accept the current conditions in our present life. This is the foundation which we're going to stand upon while we move into new lives.

We are going to Live Large right here and now, in our present circumstances.

We shall expand our Love and embody the One Heart wherever we are.

It's as if we were archers and we wanted to send forth our arrows as far as possible. The first thing that we have to do is pull back the bow towards ourselves, away from the direction that we want the arrow to travel. When we do this, we are pulling in our energies back to our Core Self while accepting our present circumstances as our launching pads into the future. This act of Accepting the Unacceptable & realigning our beings to our Core Selves creates the momentum that propels us forward. We don't need to be freed *from* our present circumstances, rather we need to become free *within* them. This is how they will transform.

Here's part of my story to illustrate what I mean:

I began Star-Borne in 1987 and for several years had done most of the work myself. This included writing books, organizing workshops, traveling, giving talks & workshops, designing fliers, writing our newsletter, sending out orders, and paying the bills. At the same time, I had my children to take care of. In 1990 Star-Borne began expanding. By 1991, I was traveling all over the world to prepare people for the 11:11 Activation. Star-Borne rapidly grew to eleven full-time, dedicated employees and numerous volunteers, most of whom had never done this type of work before. The phones were ringing day and night. The office finally moved out of my home into a large space in town. We even opened a starry store. For a few years, everything functioned fairly smoothly. Although there was a continual turnover, we had a good staff who worked together in relative harmony.

By mid 1993, Star-Borne was totally out of control. About thirty people had moved to Virginia to hang out around the energy. Everything had gotten too large and disorganized. When I was in town, I stayed home living like a hermit, writing or painting, and didn't involve myself in the activities of the "Star-Borne community." I rarely went to our office and was not involved in the daily activities of Star-Borne. When I did visit our offices, I was often made to feel unwelcome. This was interesting since Star-Borne is my company.

I was totally burnt out on office work & business responsibilities and by being constantly besieged by needy people who all wanted something from me. No matter how much I did or gave of myself, it was never enough. Most of the time I spent traveling, giving talks & workshops, so I let Star-Borne fend for itself, trusting that everything would be all right. Well, as I mentioned, it wasn't.

There was a huge cash flow which always leaked out with no tangible results. Too many people were working here; many of them doing things that I wouldn't have approved. There was the usual stuff with overblown egos, unresolved issues, latent resentments, separate agendas, etc. All I wanted was to be free of office work and business responsibilities forever! I wanted to live in an Island of Light and travel deeper into the Invisible. I also desperately wanted a personal life with a good, solid relationship, but there certainly wasn't any time or space for that.

It was obvious that something drastic needed to be done. Although I had tried to avoid Star-Borne's problems and focus on *where I really wanted to be,* the unresolved issues were still staring me in the face. So I Accepted the Unacceptable. I did the last thing that I wanted to do; the one thing I knew had to be done. I cleared out Star-Borne and brought it back into my home. Our staff was pared down to the two most dedicated & efficient people we had, plus me. I returned to work full-time in the office except for when I was traveling. I rolled up my sleeves and got back to work.

At first, this was exceedingly difficult. Every day I could feel my spirit getting crushed while I sat at my desk amidst the mountains of boring paperwork, all the letters demanding answers. Often, I would have to flee upstairs into my bedroom to regroup my energies. But I kept persevering. . . We stripped Star-Borne down to its barest essence and realigned it back into the Beam. I doggedly plugged on with as much dedication and Love as I could muster.

And you know what happened? After a short while, there were subtle changes. It became increasingly easier to work in the office. Star-Borne became clearer and more alive. My Love kept expanding. I began doing everything in new ways with very new attitudes and responses. I started having fun at work! Star-Borne kept becoming smaller and better. Soon, only two of us were managing the full load. By Accepting the Unacceptable, I was transforming my very foundation. I was bringing the New into the old, anchoring the Invisible into the physical. I was no longer stuck in my old life, doing things which I hated to do.

I had been liberated
        right in the midst
                of my old reality!

And by liberating myself, I was also freeing the things around me. Already, some of the changes that I desired in my life are starting to manifest. The elements which kept me so tightly bound are shifting into a new patterning. And I am on the brink of finally moving into something totally New!

• •

I share my story with you so perhaps, you can see how Accepting the Unacceptable brings the very changes you so desire. *We must Live Large wherever we are.* We must start doing this right now, not at some distant point in the future when the conditions are perfect. LIVING LARGE RIGHT NOW expands the present moment and allows the necessary realignment of our outer reality to happen.

THE THIRTY-SECOND KEY:

Islands of Light

Islands of Light. . .

Many of us have a deep yearning to live together in conscious Oneness.

This yearning to live in a sacred community of kindred spirits, to create a new, larger family based on Love and Oneness, is embedded deep within our cellular memory banks. It is something we have carried within us for a long, long time. It is one of our most precious dreams.

Over the years, numerous communities have been established with these goals in mind; yet most, if not all, of them have failed. There have been spiritual, religious, alternative & hippie communities which have tried to create something new. But always, there was the intrusion of duality which kept them from achieving their goal.

True Islands of Light are anchored in the Spaces-in-Between.

The true Islands of Light for which we yearn are anchored in the Invisible. This is why we haven't had any lasting success with the communities we've created. We cannot create the New if we are not New Beings. We cannot live in Oneness if we haven't already anchored our beings there. If we want to experience real Love, we must first anchor the One Heart and live with wide open hearts.

Islands of Light are definitely in our future; *they are our future.* They are the key points on this planet in the times to come—the places where the Invisible will be anchored into the physical. They are the launching pads into the Greater Reality and will serve as stabilization pinions for the entire planet during these turbulent times of the changeover from duality to Oneness. They are the seedlings of the new world which is being born. If the Earth & humanity is going to make this quantum leap into Oneness, Islands of Light must be established.

So why don't we yet have any Islands of Light? Well, just imagine that someone handed you a beautiful piece of land and lots of money to create your Island of Light. Would you be ready? Could you step out of your present life and go there right now? If not, then take a good look at what holds you back; these are your hooks into duality. They can take the form of family obligations, career responsibilities, unresolved relationships, unfulfilled desires, fears of the Unknown, feelings of unworthiness, attachments to the shimmering threads of glamour, etc. This is what you need to complete or free yourself from before you are ready to live a new life in an Island of Light.

Now I know that some of you think you are ready to leap into an Island of Light right now. You've been waiting impatiently for aeons for one to manifest. But are you really ready? Take a good look at yourself and see how much baggage you are carrying. You may have gotten rid of your physical possessions, but how much internal baggage do you still have? How's your old ego doing? Are you truly anchored in Oneness? Have you transformed your anger, fears, envy, ego, unworthiness, etc.? If you don't have your life in order right now, if your being's not in balance, then how can you go to an Island of Light? There is also a level of purification and recalibration which must be reached in order to live in the subtle energies of the Invisible. For example, Islands of Light are inappropriate places for drug and alcohol dependencies. These must be cleared up before you are ready to come. We don't want to take these old patterns with us into a new way of being.

The purpose of these new communities is not to be escapes from the harsh world of duality, but rather to be places where already free-alive-real whole beings live together as One and create something totally New. If you go to an Island of Light to escape from your duality-based personality self, you will simply bring it along with you and have to deal with it there. You don't miraculously become a new person overnight when you arrive at an Island of Light. You have to deal with your problems *before* you go to an Island of Light. You need to be a whole being already anchored in Oneness.

An Island of Light is a State of Being.

That's right, an Island of Light is a state of consciousness. If we really want to establish these wondrous communities where the Invisible and physical merge, then we must first create an Island of Light within our own beings. RIGHT HERE AND NOW. This is where the Power of the Journey comes in because it is constantly bringing us the perfect experiences we need to transform into our True Core Selves. Each of us must become an Island of Light. Then, and only then, will we be ready to unite and establish communities.

While we are undergoing this necessary transformation into Oneness, we can create Islands of Light wherever we are. If we can't be in a new place, we can make wherever we happen to be a new place. We can start living a real life, putting our full awareness into everything we do. We can BE THE LOVE wherever we are. There's nothing to wait for; do it now!

Begin with your home—wherever you are living right now. It doesn't matter if it's a mansion, a room in someone's apartment or a hut. Whatever it is, unpin it from duality. Recalibrate your surroundings; make them beautiful and sacred. Clear out the clutter and clean it up. Wash your windows and sweep your floors.

Do you have any altars? In most houses, the television set is the main focal point and serves as the unconscious altar. Set up real altars, or better yet, make your entire home an altar. Remember that altars can be subtle; they don't have to be full of candles, statues and incense. Those are the altars of the Spirituality of Duality. Creating altars is simply a conscious placement of meaningful objects which represent or embody a heightened consciousness. Flowers, a shell, anything which emanates light or aliveness and strengthens your remembrance of who you truly are.

Make your home a Neutral Zone, a place where the Invisible can be anchored. Keep it clean and clear at all times. Let it become a place of healing and nourishment for you, an oasis from the unreal world of duality.

Check to see if you have a balance of Earth & Star energies in your house. This is vitally important, for most homes have neither Earth nor Star energies present. They are synthetic, 3D, artificial worlds which flatten and dull our spirits and keep us hooked into duality. We need to be surrounded by both Earth & Star. Every room should have something which evokes both the natural world and the starry realms.

Make sure that your surroundings, as humble as they may be, make your spirit soar. Use colors that feed your being rather than deaden you. Let your home be a place of both inspiration and comfort. If you have any square objects such as tables or pyramids, turn them so they become diamonds and you'll be amazed at the shift in calibration.

Now, regard your home as an Island of Light. Live in it as if you had already arrived in your chosen community. Make every day special, a new rebirth. Sing to your house; talk to the objects around you in Star Language. Love them and feel the Love being returned by everything around you. If you do this, you will be happier than ever before and finally ready to live in an Island of Light.

Islands of Light are crucial
to the survival of the planet.

The future of this planet has yet to be determined. Much depends on us. Our future will be decided by the levels of beingness we choose to embody, by our everyday actions, by the purity of our hearts, by how real and alive we allow ourselves to be, by the foundation we stand upon. The New World is ready to be born, but it is up to us as the midwives of this birth, to bring it into being. There is no-one else to do it for us.

In order to fully anchor the Invisible into the physical, there must be anchoring points to serve as stabilization pinions and insertion points for the Greater Reality to enter. These are the Islands of Light and this is why we carry this dream within our hearts.

THE THIRTY-THIRD KEY:

Vibrantly Alive!

Vibrantly Alive!. . .

Every moment is the chance of a lifetime!

We die and are reborn daily. Each new day gives us wondrous opportunities to start fresh, to live in new ways as a New Being. It doesn't matter if the outer conditions are the same as before. WE ARE NEW! We are now freed to live our lives with our integrity intact, to LIVE LARGE and LOVE LARGE wherever we are.

All the old outer forms have been stretched wide open. They have expanded so the New can be born. The best stance we can now take is to remain open and undefined, to surf on the waves of the Invisible. The Big Waves are here and they are leading us to where we most need to go. So, relax and enjoy the ride.

Every action we make, whether it be large or small, is determining our future. Each response, habit or attitude sets up a resonance which aligns us into a similar patterning. If we stay wide open and undefined, we can align our beings with the Greater Harmonic. We can become Vibrantly Alive.

Living Large is a continual process. Each time that we expand our vastness, we must bring it into the body, integrating our vastness into every cell. Our physical bodies always travel with us into the Invisible. We are like works in progress, ever transforming, ever being recalibrated and renewed. One of the ways we do this is to constantly expand our Inner Sanctums.

Expanding your Inner Sanctum

Go into the deepest place within your being, to your most private Inner Sanctum. Enter this sacred sanctuary and center yourself there. This is the secret place within you where no-one goes and few ever touch. Perhaps, even you do not know this place well. This is the core of your being, the most intimate depths of your soul.

Now, slowly expand your Inner Sanctum outwards, unfolding it like the petals of a flower. Peel it out until it extends outwards to all your extremities. Then look inside and you will discover that a new Inner Sanctum has been revealed. Even you were not aware of this new Inner Sanctum, for it could not be revealed until the old one was expanded. Sit in the center of this new private place and feel the new depths of your being. Now, expand this Inner Sanctum outwards, adding more petals to the flower of your being. And a deeper Inner Sanctum will be revealed. . .

Remember to continually repeat this process and you will be able to access previously undiscovered parts of yourself. This is one of the ways that we can expand our beings as we travel through the unexplored realms of the deeper Invisible. In the Template of Duality we stayed in a static position with our Inner Sanctum. We thought that it was our greatest depth, our internal core. But there is so much more. . .

Welcome to the New Normal!

Here are some elements found in the New Normal:

• Permanent Surrender •

We are in a constant state of wide open surrender. We have no more control, nor do we want any. We are surfing on the waves of the Invisible. And we know that the waves will take us exactly where we need to go.

• Continuous Leap Mode •

We are ready to make quantum leaps at any time. Our belief systems are stretched wide open, ready to be continually expanded. Watch for those inserts into the Greater Reality, and when they appear, stop everything else & LEAP!

• New Beginnings •

Whenever you arrive at a new place, always pay attention to the people you first meet & the places you are drawn to. They contain important seeds for your future.

• Living Large is Fun! •

If you're not having fun, then you need to become even Larger. Living Large is *always* fun. Be playful, take things lightly & enjoy the ride!

• An Enhanced SO WHAT! •

As you live your life, learn to observe it with enlarged detachment. When the big challenges come, learn to meet them with an enhanced attitude of SO WHAT! Do your best and flow right through them.

We are setting the templates for our future now!

The key is in the present moment, not in some far off future. The key is *who you are right now,* who you embody in daily life, not who you would like to be or your untapped potential. It's *who you are right now* that is setting the templates for your future.

We can choose to be Alive right now, *in this very moment.* We can put our full being into everything we do. We can live our lives with unbridled openheartedness. We can become wild, natural and free! We don't have to wait any longer for the ideal conditions; *we can do it right now!* The New World is here; all we have to do is enter it...

Living in the New Matrtix

The mesh of our old Matrix has stretched wide open. By being true to our Core Beings, we are catapulted into a new weaving of Oneness. Everything is being profoundly realigned, revealing a New World. Something stirs deep within us, quickening our very cells. It is the spark of life! And for the first time, we become Vibrantly Alive. Alive like never before—alert—awake—fearless—Loving. We have grounded our vastness into our enlivened physical forms. We are unified Earth-Star Beings anchored in the One Heart.

Now it is time to live with our full beings, ecstatically alive. We are finally free! Free to be our unfettered Selves. Free to enter a totally New World...

A Fable For Our Time. . .

Our journey up the mountain of duality has been a long one. It began at the dawn of time and continues until the end of time. How many sunsets until the New Dawn arises?

We have stumbled and fallen many times. Bruised and battered, weakened by doubts and fears, we always manage to get up and continue on. Sometimes our journey goes quickly—images pass by in a blur. Caught up in the excited anticipation of something New, our pace quickens. Sometimes it is painfully slow—one foot doggedly placed in front of the other, like slogging through thick mud.

Along the way we have picked up many useful skills and bits of wisdom. We have learned some of the tricks of this 3D world. We know how to balance a checkbook and drive a car. We can navigate our way through crowded shopping malls and busy highways. We can discuss knowledgeably the latest political crisis or celebrity scandal. Our brilliant invention of money has taught us the difference between rich and poor. We know that if we accumulate enough money, we can amass more material goods, making us a better person, bringing us temporary happiness.

We have ordered our lives in a precise neatness. Keeping everything defined and in its proper place. We have divided up our planet into lots of little countries, allotting each their own unique culture. We have assigned roles to everyone whom we encounter. Creating innumerable boundaries so that everything can be contained in a tidy little world.

On our journey up the mountain we had to walk through the world of nature. It was simply too wild and unpredictable. Something had to be done or it would slow us down. So with our finest man-made skills, we started exerting control over the environment as best we could. Our modern technology really helped us out here. So did our voracious appetite for increasing amounts of natural resources. Species started dying out—but perhaps, they were already obsolete. Anyway, we no longer had enough space to allow them undisturbed habitats. Old forest giants who held our planetary matrix were indiscriminately chopped down. Wasn't our need for lumber greater than this? Weather patterns were tampered with, all in the name of progress. All the while, we prided ourselves on our cleverness. We were humans and humans were in power on this planet!

While we were creating such marvels of progress and advanced technology, we walked on a trail littered with broken hearts. Earth became a planet of broken hearts. We all yearned for Love, yet had no idea what it was. All we had to work with was a tiny, distorted module containing rigid, predefined, limited concepts of love. We were small beings trying desperately to love with even smaller hearts. And what pain we all experienced in the name of love.

Back at the beginning, we structured distinct tribal groups to keep our bloodlines pure and help us remember why we were here. When that finally failed, we fell back on tightly closed family units. We had created another limiting structure to define our closest relationships. Again, we assigned everyone proscribed roles and expected everything to proceed in an orderly fashion.

But, it did not. For we soon discovered that this didn't fulfill us. Something was missing. There was a huge, gaping hole in our lives that filled us with the worse discontent.

Something was terribly wrong. Nevertheless, we continued trudging up the mountain, trying to shake off the all-pervading sense of emptiness which clung to us no matter what.

We began our search for meaning. Trying to find quick comfort in a belief system that would allow us to maintain our established ways and avoid change. But there was no comfort here. Scattered around the planet, inspired individuals sought out a Higher Truth. They fasted, went on vision quests, took magical potions—anything to alter their consciousness and bring a greater understanding. Revelations were received and from these, religions were founded. Now we all had somewhere to go, something to believe in. We didn't have to discover the truth of existence for ourselves; someone else had already done it for us. How easy it seemed until we found out that secondhand knowledge was hollow. This filled us with an even greater emptiness than before.

Thrust back into the emptiness, back into our own selves, we continued our solitary trek up the mountain of duality. This brings us to our present lifetime when humanity began to quantum leap. There was a great spiritual awakening. The Fourth Dimension was anchored, and then the Fifth. Doors opened and worlds began tumbling down. Duality itself began to dissolve. Everything which we had created and established started to fall apart. All our great institutions, our modes of doing things, ways of living, established belief systems, our understanding of love have been shown to be ineffective and unenlightened. They are ridden with holes, infested with the worms of decay and corruption.

There is a New World waiting for us.

Along the way, we have shed so many layers, recalibrated our very cells, stripped ourselves to the core. Surrendered everything again and again. We have learned to Love with One Heart, embracing everything, everyone, in Oneness. Reclaiming our Core Selves, we are being reborn.

Finally, the summit of the mountain is in sight. We will soon be there. Now, we have almost reached the end of time, the final sunset of duality. We know that whatever lies ahead will be totally different than anything we have known before.

Let's walk the last few steps to the summit together. Each step we take sets us freer. Each step takes us deeper into the Greater Reality. Feel the final layers dissolve as YOU finally emerge. An Earth-Star Being. Clear and serene. Real & Vibrantly Alive!

We are the New World.
It is here and it is now!

The Invisible gently anchors into the physical, transforming everything. Duality dissolves. Islands of Light are formed where we can live together in heightened frequencies of Oneness. Planet Earth experiences a massive expansion of the Greater Love.

The Big Question. . .

Was this all just a fanciful dream, an unrealized potential, or do we really make this quantum leap into Oneness? Do we birth a New World? The answer is up to YOU!

A
Greater
Reality
Check

It's time for a

GREATER
REALITY
CHECK.

The One is Having A Great Day,

Are You?

•

The One always has a great day.

If you're not, why not?

The GREATER Checklist

Here's a list of some important components in our lives. It's not a comprehensive list, so feel free to add to it. Try to rate them on a scale of 1 to 11. When you're finished, look carefully at the results. Low numbers will signify areas of compromise, limitation, unfulfilled desires or false *security*. Now, see how you can transform these elements to better reflect your Core Self. . .

✓ **My Core Self:**
Am I being true to my Self at all times?
Do I know my Core Self?
Do I approve of myself?
Am I open to change?
Am I willing to quantum leap?
Am I willing to undo my old belief systems
to accelerate change?
Do I give myself time to be quiet and alone?
Do I feel Love when I am alone?
Do I nourish myself?
Do I speak my truth?
Am I gentle with myself?
Am I playful?
Do I have outlets to express my creativity?
Do I express my power cleanly?
Do I cover my Core Self with assumed roles?
Do I allow myself to be raw, stripped & vulnerable?

REALITY

✓ **My Physical Body:**
    Do I love my body?
    Do I accept it just the way it is?
    Do I give it regular exercise?
    Do I help make it more beautiful?
    Do I feel at ease in my body?
    Do I feel Vibrantly Alive?
    Do I dress to express my True Self?
    Have I unified Earth & Star within my body?

✓ **My Intimate Relationships:**
    Have I unified my inner polarities of Sun & Moon?
    Do my intimate relationships clearly reflect who I am?
    Am I in partnership with someone who is my equal?
    Can I openly show my Core Self?
    Can I wholeheartedly express my Love?
    Can I receive my partner's Love?
    Am I stimulated in this relationship?
    Do I feel natural with my partner?
    Do I feel safe with my partner?
    Do we share the same level of awareness?
    Do we have similar goals?
    Do we have similar value systems?
    Are we supportive of each others' growth?
    Am I open & honest with my partner?
    Does my partner inspire my creativity?

Do I feel safe being vulnerable with my partner?
Can we communicate deeply?
Do we have fun together?
Do we both share the responsibilities?
Are we aligned on the physical, mental, emotional &
spiritual levels?

✓ My Relationships with Friends, Family & Co-Workers:

(You might want to rate each of these categories separately.)

Do I openly show my True Being?
Am I honest in my dealings with others?
Do I meet these people in the One Heart?
Can I show my vulnerability?
Can I show my strength?

✓ My Career:

Am I doing work that fulfills me?
Do I constantly give my best?
Does my job stimulate my creativity?
Am I happy in my career?
Am I doing what I really want to do?
Am I honest?
Do I have integrity in all my dealings?

✓ My Heart's Desires:

Am I aware of the desires of my heart?
Do I feel that it's important to fulfill them?
Am I on the road to fulfilling my heart's desires?

✓ My Home Environment:

Is my home a clear reflection of my inner being?
Do I keep my home clean?

Do I have altars in my home?
Do I feel nourished by my home environment?
Is it highly calibrated?
Is it a Neutral Zone?
Do I communicate with the objects around me?
Do I communicate with my plants?
Do I sleep well there?
Is it anchored in Oneness?
Do I feel safe in my home?
Is it beautiful?
If not, why not?
Do I continually recalibrate the energies of my home?

✓ My Day-to-Day Life:
Am I happy to be on this planet?
Am I grounded?
Do I see that everything I do is sacred?
Is my heart open?
Do I achieve my everyday tasks joyfully?
Do I greet each day as a new being?

✓ My Aspirations & Goals:
Am I aware of my aspirations and goals?
Do I follow them?
Am I open to revise them?

✓ Surfing:
Do I remember to check the condition of the waves?
Do I regularly practice the GO?
Do I align myself with the Waves of the Invisible?
Have I let go of control?
Do I trust the waves?

The GREATER REALITY
Troubleshooting Guide

Check Your Connections:

The first thing that all Troubleshooting Guides ask is to check your connections. Are you correctly plugged into the power system? In this case, we would ask:

1. Are you doing the GO?

2. Have you anchored your being into the Earthstar?

3. Are you standing in the Beam?

4. Is your One Heart activated?

5. Have you merged Earth & Star?

6. Now, instead of plugging yourself in, unhook yourself from duality and unpin yourself from time and space.

If your problems persist, please read on for some potential adjustments.

A Checklist of Potential Adjustments:

✓ Your Core Self:

Who are you really? Who do you embody in daily life? Is it your duality-based personality or your Core Self? Are you stripped to the Core? If not, why not? Perhaps, it's time to remove some of the padding which surrounds your Core Self. Be courageous! Dare to be raw, vulnerable, tender, real and alive!

✓ Your Aspirations & Value Systems:

Let's take a good, hard look at your Goals in life. What's truly important to you? What do you consider the most important thing for you to achieve in your lifetime? What things do you value the most? Which qualities? What aspirations? Is your present value system anchored in duality or Oneness? What do you need to readjust?

✓ Your Commitment:

Have you made a firm commitment to anchor your being in Oneness and be Vibrantly Alive? Are you prepared to go the full distance? Are you ready to step off the map of the known into the Invisible? If not, why not? What holds you back?

✓ Anger:

Anger is actually a most useful tool. Lessons abound each time we become angry. It reveals our weak spots, the places where we get snagged in duality. Anger is an alarm system which shows us the places which most need healing and transformation. Study well the triggers which set off your anger. They reflect your predominant, unresolved issues.

Anger gives us a much needed lesson in empowerment; each time we become angry we give our power away. Don't be afraid of your anger or lock it up in denial. Become familiar with the core energy behind it. If you remain balanced, centered and anchored in Oneness, you can utilize this core energy in positive ways. It will give you the momentum to accomplish things, to create, to be strong.

Anger is aligned with the four elements of Earth, Water, Fire & Air, and manifests uniquely in each element. Earth & Water Anger are less dramatic, but more long lasting. Fire & Air Anger pass quickly. Earth & Air Anger are cold and unemotional. Water & Fire Anger are full of emotions.

Earth Anger:
A slow, hardened toughness which shows itself as intractable stubbornness. Cold, immovable, unloving, long lasting. The person with Earth Anger doesn't want to discuss it. The root cause of their anger is frustration and anger with themselves.

Water Anger:
A silent, moody, long lasting, emotional anger full of resentment, jealousy & envy which spreads and oozes all around the surrounding area like a heavy fog. The person with Water Anger denies anything is wrong and doesn't want to discuss it.

Fire Anger:
An explosive, sometimes volatile, always dramatic anger. Fire Anger is the type of anger which most frightens people because of its raw force and magnitude. It's the most openly destructive type of anger. However, it can also be a very clean anger. When the explosion passes, it is gone. The person with Fire Anger gets angry quickly and uncontrol-

lably when they are triggered. After the blast of anger, they
soon return to normal.

Air Anger:

An anger like the wind which impartially strips away any
blockages or illusions. Air Anger is clean and unemotional.
It comes from the realms of mind and is often used to de-
fend cherished ideals or concepts. The person with Air
Anger lets go of their anger as easily as they picked it up.

There is also a constructive form of anger which acts much
like a Stripping Wind. This type of anger has no meanness;
it is simply raw energy which is utilized to sear away and
purify whatever needs to be cleansed or clarified. Constructive Anger is expressed as either Fire or Air Anger.

✔ Depression-Compression:

When you feel depressed or when the energies build up
into an immensely heavy pressure which feels like it's going to compress you, then that's a sure sign that you need
to make a big change. The only solution is to Surrender.
Surrender everything and watch as you quickly move from
breakdown to breakthrough.

✔ Fears of the Unknown:

Are you still clinging to your old restrictions, roles and limitations and calling them "security"? Are you afraid to let
go of outdated belief systems and enter a phase of not
knowing? Are you acting like a fly on a window? Have you
noticed how flies like to congregate on the inside of a window. They are filled with longing to go outside. Right next
to their window is an open door, their assured passage to
the destination they wish to reach. They will often remain
pressed against the window gazing at the world they want
to enter until the day they die. And yet, all they have to do

is alter their perspective and go in a new direction and they will find their way to a larger world, the world that calls them.

If you are held back by your Fears of the Unknown, then simply accept that the Unknown is unknowable. That there undoubtedly will be some discomfort and awkwardness while we are changing our reality systems. And that since we are traveling off the map of the known, none of us knows what we will find. Fears of the Unknown are a normal occurrence; we all have them from time to time. It's part of the journey. Accept your fears and carry on.

✓ Forgiveness:

Are you still holding on to deep resentments, old hurts and betrayals? If so, it's time to let them go. FORGIVE everyone, FORGIVE all past experiences, and FORGIVE YOURSELF! Everything that happened in your life was absolutely perfect. It brought you limitless opportunities to grow and learn. Let go, embrace your new freedom, and go on.

✓ Fried in the Beam:

This condition occurs when we have been too immersed in the accelerated energies without giving ourselves time for grounding and integration. We feel extremely raw, seared, pulsating, wild eyed. When this happens, take a break. Pull the plug for a while and go on a picnic. Do something fun! Focus on the simple and mundane. Clean your house; work in the garden, take walks, play with your cats, watch movies. Get physical and stay busy. If that doesn't work, take a long bubblebath, then go to bed with a stack of magazines and a box of chocolates. Soon you'll be healed and ready for another dose of accelerated energies.

✓ Function Shutdown:

Symptoms of Function Shutdown include an inability to think, act, and love. You don't want to eat or interact with anyone. Often, all you can do is sleep or wander about in a hopeless daze. Actually, this isn't as bad as it sounds. Function Shutdown has two possible causes. Sometimes, we are shut down when we are doing some huge task on another plane of existence which takes all of our energy. Or it may occur while we are undergoing a massive repatterning. Whenever you experience Function Shutdown, simply accept it. Do as little as possible. Remain quiet and inactive until it passes and you can function again.

✓ Hooks of Duality:

Duality is like a rubber band; it keeps on pulling us back. Remember, it needs us to make it real. Without our participation, duality will cease to exist. So, even if we have made a firm and unwavering commitment to anchor ourselves in Oneness, we can expect duality to repeatedly attempt to get us back. The way it does this is to find those places where we are still hooked into duality and yank on them. This can be quite helpful actually, for it reveals where our hooks are located. It shows us what we can work on to become freer.

The challenge is to remain ultra conscious of our hooks so that when they are yanked, we're not pushed back into the sticky realms of duality. If you can remain aware of what is happening while you are hooked back into duality, you're well onto the road of freedom. Suspend self judgment and remember that we all experience being pulled back into duality's clutches from time to time. It's a useful practice which allows us to develop greater mastery.

After we become aware of the existence of our hooks into

duality, the next step is to get rid of them. Gently unhook yourself each time you find one. This may entail some drastic action like letting go of an unhealthy relationship, changing your job, or making a gigantic surrender of everything. Do whatever it takes. Get yourself free! Each time you discover a hook, take it out. Change that situation or change your response to that situation. Adjust your attitudes; drop those judgements. Shift your value system, whatever.

✔ Jammed Controls:

Have all your well laid plans fallen apart? Have you lost your highly esteemed sense of control? Are you being helplessly swept along by the waves of the Invisible? Congratulations! Your old controls have jammed. This means that you are progressing nicely. Now, let go of your last vestige of *wanting* to be in control, and enjoy the ride.

✔ Love Drought:

If you're feeling a massive lack of love in your life then it's time to get back into the One Heart. *BE THE LOVE.* Start nourishing and loving yourself. Remember that Sacred Union is taking place around you all the time. Leap into this Sea of Love. Be Loving to everyone whom you encounter. See how everything and everyone is expressing their Love to you. Love nature and show your Love to the objects around you. Jump into the subtle currents of Sacred Union. Become a true Master of Love.

✔ Overstressed Mind:

So, you've been thinking too much. . . Hmm, it must be time to send your 3D mind off on a holiday and live without it for a while. Stop thinking and analyzing everything! Every time you start to reactivate that old chattering, monkey mind of yours, move into your heart. FEEL. LOVE. ACT. BE. Just don't think. Stop reading until this state passes.

Stop trying to understand. FEEL. Keep refocusing on Love. Feel that Sacred Union taking place all around. Get physical and keep yourself busy, fully focusing on each task.

✓ Polarization:

When the old *"us"* versus *"them"* strikes, you've entered the murky zone of Polarization where there always has to be a winner and a loser. We endlessly bounce back and forth between these two poles, often getting banged up in the process. While it feels great to temporarily be the winner, we know that sooner or later the scales are going to shift and we'll be going down, down. In duality, everything has its opposite. There's always the two sides of the coin. So if we're happy, that means that we'll have to pay for that by being sad. If something good happens, then something bad will happen to balance out our good fortune. And so it goes when Polarization is present. Since Polarization is one of the cornerstones of duality, we have grown to accept this as a basic reality. Well, it's not anymore!

When we are anchored in Oneness, we are freed from the grip of Polarization. We can step out of the outmoded roles of winner and loser as we discover that there is always a Graceful Solution to everything! A Graceful Solution is a Win-Win situation where everyone is benefited. It's always present. There is *always* a Graceful Solution, even to the most challenging problems. All you have to do is know that it's there and don't settle for anything less. Look for the Graceful Solution and you will find it. This is a basic precept of the Template of Oneness.

✓ Random Weirdness:

These are seemingly inexplicable, unexpected happenings in our life which appear to have no basis in reality. *For example:* Suddenly, a good friend disappears out of your life.

You didn't even have an argument. Nothing bad happened between you. Yet, all of a sudden, they are gone. Sure, you can call them, but they will never return your calls. They'll never want to see you again. But there's no good reason for this rupture. Yes, there is, it's Random Weirdness. *Here's another example:* You have a business and you've been working successfully with another company for years. Now, they don't want to work with you any longer. And if you do work together, they mess up all the work, miss your deadlines and are generally uncooperative. But why? Random Weirdness is the only answer.

Having experienced too much Random Weirdness over the past several years, I have diligently searched for an explanation. Perhaps, it is due to the accelerated energies of this highly unusual time we are in. Random Weirdness is an insert imposed into our present reality to move people and things around into their proper positioning. It helps us shift from our old positions in the Template of Duality to our new positioning in the Template of Oneness. Although it is perplexing when it strikes, Random Weirdness is a gift that always brings us greater perfection. Whenever Random Weirdness strikes, don't fight it. Accept the surprising changes and get ready to move in a new direction.

✓ Squawky Fragments:

Are there several aspects of yourself which are in conflict? Do you feel pulled in many directions at once? Are you uncertain as to which aspect you should listen to? Do you have trouble making decisions? If so, it's certainly time to gather all the dispersed fragments of your being together in One Being.

Each fragment of our being brings us something we need to become whole. If they are being squawky, find out what they want. Why are they trying to get your attention? During our life's journey we continually encounter stranded or abandoned fragments of our being. Some of them were left behind in the locations of past lives. Others became attached to another person or to a cause. Some, we simply shut away because we weren't ready to deal with them yet. All of these fragments need to be embraced into our greater One Being. Your fragments are like a team of wild horses. They need to be hitched together to the wagon of your One Being; then hand the reins over to your Core Self.

✓ Stagnation:
Are you sick of the *same old, same old?* Do you feel that nothing new is coming into your life? Perhaps, this is because you are too full. Our beings are like chalices. If we keep them filled to the brim, this leaves no room for the entrance of something new. If your chalice is filled with old sludge, how can you pour in the sparkling Elixir of the New? So empty out some of that old useless stuff that's been accumulating. Strip your being; strip your house; strip your activities and relationships. Keep only what's really true and alive. Make room for the New!

✓ Stunted Relationships:
If you are still involved in dysfunctional relationships, it's time to take a good, clear look at yourself. What is it within you which still holds onto this pattern of imbalance? Why do you allow yourself to be in limited, confining, unhealthy relationships? What are you afraid of? Where are your attachments in these situations? Is your responsibility to this relationship based on guilt or karma? Do you feel unworthy of real Love? Stunted Relationships have no place in our future. They don't serve any of the parties involved. Find a graceful way to complete them and step into freedom.

Map of the 11:11

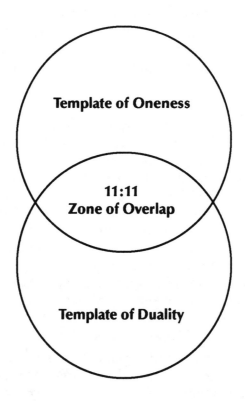

Template of Oneness

11:11
Zone of Overlap

Template of Duality

Map of the Antarion Conversion

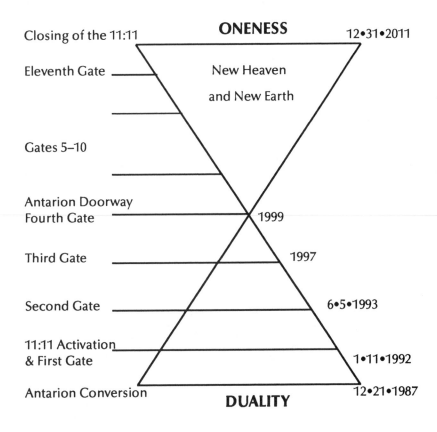

Closing of the 11:11   **ONENESS**   12•31•2011

Eleventh Gate

New Heaven
and New Earth

Gates 5–10

Antarion Doorway
Fourth Gate   1999

Third Gate   1997

Second Gate   6•5•1993

11:11 Activation
& First Gate   1•11•1992

Antarion Conversion   **DUALITY**   12•21•1987

The Star-Borne Dictionary

Since we use language a little differently than most people, here's a most helpful dictionary of some of our key phrases. These phrases were created when we were faced with the supreme challenge of communicating the unexplainable and found no words to explain the energies we were experiencing. To put things into their proper perspective, we've also included and *redefined*, some of the more popular spiritual concepts within the Template of Duality.

This Glossary will also be helpful to those who seek a more esoteric explanation of the energies we are experiencing in our daily lives. However, it's not necessary to understand this in order to Live Large. Living Large is an extremely practical, day-to-day merger of the Invisible and the physical.

11:11:

11:11 is a pre-encoded trigger placed in our cellular memory banks prior to our descent into matter which when activated, signifies that our time of completion and ascension is near. We are graduating from duality and rising into Oneness. This number has mysteriously and persistently appeared to millions of people around the world, awakening them to the significance of these present times. It is a powerful catalyst to remembrance. The Master Number Eleven by itself is a herald of the New and the Unknown. The double Elevens signify a supra-normal occurrence emanating from a new sector of awareness. In this case, the double Elevens announce the opening of the entrance into the Greater Reality.
See also: Doorway of the 11:11, Greater Reality, Master Numbers.
Recommended Reading: *11:11–Inside the Doorway, The Star-Borne.*

Akashic Records:

The storehouse or Great Hall of Records of all knowledge and experiences accumulated within the Template of Duality. The Akashic Records are available for everyone. Mechizedek oversees the hidden wisdom within the Great Hall of Records. It is located on the Star System Mensa in the constellation of the Triangle. However, the Akashic Records are only useful to us while we are evolving on the spiral of duality. Once we enter the Unknown, we are traveling on an entirely new map.
See also: Spirals of Evolution, Template of Duality, Unknown.

All-Encompassing Love:

The entry level of Love found within the Template of Oneness. All-Encompassing Love is all inclusive; nothing is separate from the One. There is no more "I" or "you"; we are all part of the One. We all share the same heart, which is the One Heart.
See also: One Heart, Template of Oneness, Unconditional Love.

All-Seeing Eye of AN:

The apex of seeing within the Template of Duality. Seeing moves beyond our physical eyes and third eye to utilize the entire head as well as the space around our head. This enables us to see into the preliminary levels of the Invisible.
See also: AN, Triangulation.

AN:

The Sacred Union of the Sun & Moon into One Being. *Also:* The merger of male and female polarities into Oneness which occurs within our own beings. *Also:* An ancient, great star lineage which corresponds with the central star in the belt of Orion presently called Al Nilam. Many of us are part of the Family of AN. The elders of AN are called the Annutara. Some of them walk among us today. The Council of the Annutara was first brought to Earth in 1992. The symbol for AN used to be a Sun above a reclining crescent Moon. But since the Activation of the Second Gate in 1993, this symbol has changed and the upright crescent Moon is now found within the Sun. They now share the same eye.

Ancient Usage: AN was an early God of Sun & Moon as One Being in ancient Egypt. The Temple of AN was located in Heliopolis which is now a part of Cairo. The priests of AN also built Stonehenge at a later time. The Tower of Light of AN was located in the Andes Mountains of Peru. Civilizations created by AN have similar characteristics: they worship the Sun & Moon and are ruled by husband and wife who are also brother and sister.
See also: An-Nu-Ta-Ra Hu, Family of AN, One Being, Sacred Union, Second Gate.

Angel Names:

The names of our Higher Selves.
See also: Angels, Star Language, Starry Names.

Angels:

Angels serve as our entry point into our own inherent vastness. After we contact our Guardian Angel, we realize that our Guardian Angel is our own Higher Self. Then we become the Angel we truly are. This is our first step into conscious Oneness. Angels are intermediaries between spirit and matter. The Angelic Realm does not exist in the heightened resonance of the Greater Reality. This is because their work is now complete. They melt into Oneness and no longer need a separate identity. Once we graduate from duality, we step beyond the level in which we are personifications of anything except the One.

See also: the One, Oneness.

Recommended Reading: *Invoking Your Celestial Guardians, The Star-Borne.*

Annutara:

The Elders of the Family of AN.

See also: AN, An-Nu-Ta-Ra Hu, Family of AN, Og-Min, Starry Councils.

An-Nu-Ta-Ra Hu:

A sacred chant which evokes the Council of the Annutara. *Annutara:* Elders of the star lineage of AN. *Council of the Annutara:* Starry Council of the Family of AN now brought to Earth. *Tibetan:* Annutara—The Highest State, above which there is nothing. *Egyptian:* AN=the God of Sun & Moon as One Being, Nut=the Goddess of the Sky, Ptah=the Creator God, Ra=the Sun God.

See also: AN, EL•AN•RA, Star Lineage, Starry Council.

Antarion Conversion:

A stepping up/stepping down station for the transfer of energies located in the Zone of Overlap within the belt of Orion. This energy transfer always follows a diagonal trajectory. It also creates the Zone of Overlap by merging the energies of Light & Dark into Oneness, thus providing the key to transcend duality.

See also: EL•AN•RA, Template of Duality, Zone of Overlap.

A•Qva•La A•Wa•La:

The Healer of Emotions and Elohim of the Oceans who guides us through the watery currents of the First Gate. A•Qua•La A•Wa•La is a starry being who works closely with the whales and dolphins. She is a sister of Kwan Yin, the Goddess of Compassion and first appeared on this planet in 1988. Her main purpose on Earth is to aid us in our journey through the First Gate by helping us heal our emotions and build new emotional bodies anchored in the One Heart. Once this is achieved, she will cease to exist within these realms.
See also: First Gate.

Ascended Masters:

Guides and teachers within the Template of Duality who have ascended from the earthplane to higher planes within duality's evolutionary spiral. In the Template of Oneness we are all Ascended Masters.
See also: Spirituality of Duality, Spirals of Evolution, Template of Duality and Template of Oneness.

Ascension:

Ascension is simply the shift in consciousness from duality to Oneness. It is the quantum leap from the evolutionary spiral of duality to that of Oneness.
See also: Oneness, Spirals of Evolution, Template of Duality, Template of Oneness.

the Beam:

This refers to direct alignment with the One. *For example:* Alignment with the Beam=embodying Oneness. Surfing the Beam=surfing the waves of the Invisible, Seared in the Beam=receiving penetrating, concentrated doses of Oneness. Fried in the Beam=our beings are overloaded with accelerated frequencies. Part One of the GO is a practice to align yourself in the Beam.
See also: GO.

Beyond the Beyond:

This refers to the sector of the Unknown located within the Template of Oneness.
See also: Template of Oneness, Unknown.

Birdstar:

A flock of small white birds flying in the formation of one large white bird. The symbol of our Unified Presence, us as One. Our One Being who goes through the Doorway of the 11:11. The Birdstar is sometimes referred to as the Dove, although it is not really a dove. *Also:* It represents the Zone of Overlap or place of merging where bird and star become indistinguishable. This is the Sacred Union of Earth & Star. The inverse of the Birdstar is the Starbird which is birthed by turning our One Being inside out after we have passed through the 11:11. The Starbird is our vehicle to travel on the far side of the 11:11, once we have entered the Greater Reality.
See also: Doorway of the 11:11, Greater Reality, One Being, Zone of Overlap.

Chakras:

Spiritual energy centers located in the physical body within the Template of Duality. They are unified into the One Heart in the Template of Oneness.
See also: One Heart, Template of Duality, Template of Oneness.

Core Self:

Our true, stripped down, no frills, basic Essence. It is wide open, raw, tender and vulnerable. We need to stand in our Core Self in order to birth our New Selves.

Divine Intervention:

In the Template of Duality: Divine Intervention is unexpected help from On High. Here, we often serve as Instruments of Divine Intervention. *In the Template of Oneness:* We are in a constant state of Divine Intervention. Everything is Divine Intervention. It is the natural order.
See also: Template of Duality, Template of Oneness.

Doorway of the 11:11:

A bridge between two very different evolutionary spirals, one anchored in duality, the other in Oneness. This doorway was created by overlapping and interlocking the two spirals during the Activation of the 11:11 which took place on January 11, 1992. Over a hundred thousand people participated worldwide in groups large and small. The two Master Cylinders were located at the Great Pyramids in Egypt—the Omega Point and in Queenstown, New Zealand—the Alpha Point.

The Doorway of the 11:11 opens once and closes once, and only One may pass through. This is a reference to the fact that we graduate from duality by uniting into conscious Oneness and becoming One Being. The 11:11 is scheduled to close on December 31, 2011. At this time, the two spirals of evolution will separate. The choice before us is whether we want to anchor our beings in duality or in Oneness.

See also: 11:11, Birdstar, EL•AN•RA, Eleven Gates, First Gate, One Being, Oneness, Second Gate, Spirals of Evolution, Third Gate, Zone of Overlap.

Earthstar:

The Earthstar is located in the center of our planet. It represents the heart of matter, our primordial core. This point is utilized in grounding our vastness into the physical.
See also: GO.

Earth-Star:

It is important to be as intimately connected with the physical, earthy part of ourselves as we are with our vastness, personified as the Star above. Earth & Star have long been perceived to be two separate points defining the parameters of our beings and of our predominant paradigm. However, as we increasingly step into Oneness, we merge Earth & Star by quickening the Spaces-in-Between with Sacred Union. This process turns our previous parameters inside out and we transform into a vaster One Being. The term Earth-Star refers to our new unified wholeness.
See also: Earthstar, Earth-Star Dance, One Being, Oneness, Sacred Union, Spaces-in-Between.

Earth-Star Dance:

A Sacred Dance in which we embody both Earth & Star Beings. The purpose of this dance is to merge these two polarities of ourselves back into One Being.
See also: Earth-Star, One Being & Sacred Dances.

Ecstatic Love:

A state of vibrantly alive, pulsating, blissful Love producing a profound state of sublime ecstasy found within the subtle realms of the Invisible. Ecstatic Love quickens and recalibrates our very cells into the enhanced frequencies of the Greater Love. This Love originates in the One Heart. It cannot be experienced with our old emotional bodies.
See also: Greater Love, Lovers from Beyond the Stars, One Heart.

EL•AN•RA:

The three stars in the belt of the Constellation of Orion which serve as the key control points or pins to hold our dimensional universe into positional alignment within the Template of Duality. It is by merging all polarities back into Oneness, that we transcend the illusion of duality and are freed to move onwards into the Invisible. This creates a Zone of Overlap between the polarities of Light and Dark. This Zone of Overlap is anchored in Oneness. The central star in Orion's belt, currently called Al Nilam, corresponds to AN and is a black hole. It is the entry point to the Doorway of the 11:11.

Also: EL•AN•RA refers to the three great star lineages of EL, AN & RA which helped colonize this planet. These star lineages are the overseers of our journey through the evolutionary spiral of duality and our subsequent ascension into Oneness. We are intimately connected with these star lineages.
See also: AN, Doorway of the 11:11, Oneness, Template of Duality, Template of Oneness.
Recommended Reading: The Star-Borne, EL•AN•RA: The Healing of Orion & 11:11–Inside the Doorway.

Eleven Gates:

The eleven frequency bands of energy through which we must travel to complete our journey through the Doorway of the 11:11. Each Gate represents a level of awareness with which we must align ourselves before traveling further. Each Gate also has a keynote, or harmonic resonance associated with particular initiations, lessons, and recalibrations of energy.
See also: Doorway of the 11:11, First Gate, Second Gate, Third Gate.

Family of AN:

Those belonging to the star lineage of AN.
See also: AN, Annutara, EL•AN•RA.

First Gate:

The First Gate was activated simultaneously with the Doorway of the 11:11 in January, 1992. Its keynote is the healing of the heart and the creation of a new emotional body anchored in the One Heart.
See also: A•Qua•La A•Wa•La, Doorway of the 11:11, Eleven Gates, One Heart.

Fourth Dimension:

A dimension of consciousness within the Template of Duality which was anchored on Earth during the Harmonic Convergence Planetary Activation on August 16th & 17th, 1987. Its major significance is that it is a doorway to multiple dimensions.
See also: Octaves.

the Future Which Never Shall Be:

Our proposed or potential futures within the Template of Duality which shall never be manifested since we are shifting spirals. On another level, these futures are all woven into the ever-present NOW.
See also: the Past That Never Was.

GO:

A three part process to align ourselves as Pillars of Light, connecting Earth & Star within our physical bodies, which produces grounding & alignment with the One while anchoring the One Heart. This process should be practiced endlessly, until it becomes our natural stance in everyday life. It is a major tool in Living Large.
See also: Earth-Star, One Heart.

Graceful Solution:

A Graceful Solution is a Win-Win solution in which everyone benefits. This replaces the old win-lose roles of Polarization found within the Template of Duality. Win-Win is a basic precept of the Template of Duality. There is *always* a Graceful Solution, even in the most challenging situations.

Great Central Sun:

The Central Sun of the Template of Duality.

Greater Central Sun:

The vastly larger Central Sun of the Template of Oneness.

Greater Central Sun Dance:

A powerful Sacred Dance in which we birth and embody the Greater Central Sun. Inside the circle of the Greater Central Sun are three central dancers who stretch open the fabric of time and space. They are surrounded by five revolving pillars.
See also: Greater Central Sun & Sacred Dances.

Greater Love:

A new level of Love which is fully birthed once the *Lovers from Beyond the Stars* reunite into One Being, creating an opening into a deeper Love called the Greater Love.
See also: Lovers from Beyond the Stars, One Being.

Greater Reality:

The heightened, supra-normal reality system of the Template of Oneness. To get there, we must journey through the Invisible and the Unknown, traveling in the Spaces-In-Between.
See also: Invisible, Spaces-in-Between, Template of Oneness, Unknown.

Horizontal Energy:

The frequency band containing second-hand knowledge which travels on a horizontal trajectory. This was our main source of learning within the Template of Duality. Reading books, learning from teachers and other people's experiences rather than having our own direct revelations and experiences. Religions are a good example of horizontal energy. *Also:* A form of energy manipulation used in the Template of Duality which is full of sly innuendo and insinuation. Rumours and malicious gossip would fall into this category as would heartless seductions.
See also: Template of Duality, Vertical Energy.

I-Await:

A state of heightened receptivity and active passivity which occurs when you have made the needed inner transformations and await the birth of the New.
See also: the New.

Invisible:

The subtle realm which we must pass through on our journey into the Greater Reality. The Invisible and the Unknown are two aspects of the same place. They are both found in the Spaces-in-Between. All of this is part of the Template of Oneness. The Invisible is the Unseen. Part of our task here on Earth is to make visible the Invisible and to anchor the Invisible into form. We do this by exploring the Invisible, developing new ways of seeing-feeling and embodying Oneness. Then we anchor this heightened vastness into our physical bodies.
See also: the Greater Reality, Spaces-in-Between, Unknown, Unseen.

Isis and Osiris:

Isis & Osiris were Gods of ancient Egypt. They were brother-sister and husband-wife. The legend of Isis & Osiris speaks of the jealousy of their brother Set and how twice he managed to kill Osiris. The first time, Set had a wooden chest made which perfectly fit Osiris' dimensions. Then while Isis was away, he lured Osiris into the chest and shut it until Osiris expired. When Isis returned, she brought Osiris back to life through the purity of her Love and her vast healing powers. Much time passed. Set waited until again Isis was gone and then he attacked and killed his brother, cutting his body up into several pieces and scattering them all about Egypt.

When Isis returned and saw what had happened, she set out to gather up all the fragments of her beloved Osiris. She found them all, save one, which was his phallus. It had been thrown into the ocean and eaten by the whales. Again with her deep Love, she brought Osiris back to life. Rising to the vast realms of spirit, they made love and conceived their son, Horus. Then Osiris declined to rule anymore in the world of men and descended to a solitary vigil in the underworld. During her many years alone, Isis kept the sacred flame of True Love alive on this planet.

In 1992 Osiris returned from the underworld, not to this duality-based world, but to the new world which is being born. In 1993, his phallus was returned by the whales who had guarded it all this time. It was physically present at the Second Gate Activation in Ecuador that same year. The phallus of Osiris symbolizes the return of true manhood to men and the embodiment of true womanhood in women, making us now ready to unite in equal, balanced partnerships. Isis & Osiris served as the Gatekeepers at the Second Gate Activation. This marked the completion of their story and their merger into One Being.
See also: Phallus of Osiris, Second Gate.

Islands of Light:

Future communities which are created in the physical while anchored in the Invisible. They are the key points for our future

endeavors, but cannot be established until we have stepped free of duality and birthed our New Selves. An Island of Light is a place to live totally in the New. They are part of the Third Gate Initiation.
See also: Third Gate.

Karma:
The law of cause and effect found within the Template of Duality. Simply put, Karma means that you will get back what you give out; for every action there's a reaction. That sooner or later, all actions will be repaid with their just rewards or punishments; and in the end, everything balances out. Karma does not exist within the Template of Oneness.
See also: Template of Duality, Template of Oneness.

Living Large:
Physically embodying our vastness on a daily basis until it becomes the New Normal.
See also: New Normal.

Lotus Dance:
A Sacred Dance symbolizing the Lotus of True Love. Two circles of dancers represent the petals of the Lotus. As they dance, they breath in and out the ever expanding Love of the One Heart. This simple dance is a powerful way of anchoring the One Heart and has been done in many countries for this purpose. It is always performed in silence. A new, vastly heightened level of this dance has recently been revealed in which the dancers consciously represent the Lovers from Beyond the Stars.
See also: Lotus of True Love, the Lovers from Beyond the Stars, One Heart, Sacred Dances.

Lotus of True Love:
The symbol for the Template of True Love which is used to represent the Love of the One Heart. The Lotus is also associated with the Egyptian Goddess Isis who played a major role in keeping the sacred flame of True Love alive throughout the cycle of

Dark Ages on this planet. *Also:* Pure Love.
See also: Isis & Osiris, Lotus Dance, One Heart, Template, True Love.

Lovers from Beyond the Stars:

They are perceived as the holders for the focus of the Greater Love within the Template of Oneness. In fact, *they are the Template for the Greater Love.* The Lovers from Beyond the Stars are two, very expanded halves of the same being. *Also:* A level of awareness and Ecstatic Love which is brought to Earth while we are passing through the Second Gate. *Also:* The Lovers from Beyond the Stars are the Master Patterning behind all the Great Lovers such as Isis & Osiris, Tristan & Isolde, Arthur & Guinevere, etc. who have kept alive the resonance of True Love throughout the ages.
See also: Greater Love, Lotus Dance, Sacred Spiral Dance, Second Gate, Template of Oneness.

Master Numbers:

The numerical units which are our entry point into the Greater Reality. Master Numbers are: 11, 22, 33, 44, 55, 66, 77, 88 & 99. Double Master Numbers such as 11:11 are insertion points for the Greater Reality to enter.
See also: 11:11.

Neutral Zone:

A place with empty, clean, open energy where the Invisible can be anchored.

the New:

This refers to the new energies emanating from the Template of Oneness.
See also: New Matrix & Template of Oneness.

New Matrix:

This is the patterning or weaving of the Greater Reality. Here we

are all interwoven together into Oneness.
See also: Greater Reality, the New, Oneness, Template of Oneness.

New Normal:
Our heightened everyday reality once we birth our New Selves and Live Large.
See also: Living Large.

New Road:
This refers to our first steps into the Invisible once we leave behind duality by reaching the end of the old road. By entering upon the New Road, we step onto a new map, into uncharted territory.
See also: Invisible.

No-Mind:

No-Space:
The state of being unpinned from the confines of space found within the Template of Oneness. There is no more separation between *here* or *there*. Due to our increased vastness, distance has been transcended.
See also: Template of Oneness.

No-Time:
The measurement of time within the Template of Oneness. The eternal moment when past, present and future merge together in the glorious NOW.

Null Zone:
A Null Zone is created when energy expands and flowers outwards, then is shattered from without, causing the previous world or reality system to collapse inwards upon itself. It breaks all the old entrenched patterns. The old, shattered worlds cannot be

restored to their original position. Null Zones can occur on a large scale, affecting many, or within your own being. They create the womb from which the New is born.
See also: the New.

Octaves:

The measurement of levels of awareness found within the Greater Reality which replaces the dimensional patterning of our present Great Central Sun System that is aligned with the Template of Duality.
See also: Fourth Dimension, Great Central Sun, Greater Reality, & Template of Duality.

Og-Min:

A brother/sisterhood of Light Beings who live in the cave heavens which exist beyond the realms of time and space. They have four fingered hands and bodies of Light. The Og-Min offer us three levels of initiation. In the first or beginning level, we are taken to visit the Halls of the Og-Min and receive direct transmissions. In the intermediate level, we receive direct experiences. In the third level, we consciously embody the Annutara. *Tibetan:* Cloud of Truth, the pure and holy realm of Truth. The highest realm from which one can still incarnate on Earth. The refrain of the Og-Min is: *No Down, No Return.*
See also: Annutara.

the One:

Within the Template of Oneness, the One is all-encompassing. Everything is part of the One. Since nothing is separate from the One, we all have direct access to everything. There is never more than One. *Also:* The higher level of what was perceived of as the Supreme Being, personified as God, in the Template of Duality.
See also: Template of Duality & Template of Oneness.

One Being:

A level of Sacred Union that takes place between two or more persons in which you become One Vaster Being.
See also: One Love.

One Eye:

A way of *seeing-feeling* into the Invisible utilizing your full being and the Spaces-in-Between.
See also: All-Seeing Eye, Invisible, Spaces-in-Between.

One Heart:

The One Heart is the heart of all. This means that we all share the same heart. The One Heart is the core of our new emotional body and supersedes our old heart chakras. It is the foundation of the Template of Oneness.
See also: All-Encompassing Love, Chakras, First Gate, GO, Template of Oneness.

One Love:

The Love of our One Being.

Oneness:

The all-pervading energy of being One.

Paradigm:

A model, map or template.

Past Lives:

Previous incarnations by a fragment of our True Being on Earth or other planets and star systems. Although they appear to have occurred within the framework of time/space, in actuality, they are all part of the vast NOW which contains both the *Past That Never Was* and the *Future Which Never Will Be.*

the Past That Never Was:

What was perceived of as our past experiences within the Template of Duality which cease to exist once we anchor our being in Oneness.
See also: the Future Which Shall Never Be.

Phallus of Osiris:

The long missing fragment of Osiris which has now been returned. This is a direct reference to the new sexuality. There is an initiation here. Men are called to set aside their lesser physical phallus and have their whole being become the Greater Phallus. This makes it possible to make Love with your entire being in the Spaces-In-Between.
See Isis & Osiris, Second Gate, Spaces-In-Between.

Probable Realities:

That which exists within our cones of past and future in the Template of Duality. Our probable realities must be turned inside out in order for the Invisible to be revealed.

Quantum Leap:

A massive beakthrough into a new level of awareness, usually achieved quickly.

Recalibrate:

To finely tune and refine one's being.

Remnant Seed:

The physical vestige, traces or signs of something which no longer exists. Some of us are the Remnant Seed, the ancient ones who carry within them the seeds of the New. So are the forest giants, the ancient trees in old growth forests; this is why it is so important to protect them. The Remnant Seed are Keepers of the Matrix.
See also: the New, & New Matrix.

Restructurization:

A process of massively transforming ourselves on the cellular level.

Sacred Dances:

Special dances brought to the Earth at this time from the Starry

Temples. They are sacred movements which birth the new energies of Oneness into our physical bodies and into the Earth. At this point, five dances have been introduced. Each one has a special purpose and is multi-leveled.

See also: Earth-Star Dance, Greater Central Sun Dance, Lotus Dance, Sacred Spiral Dance & Starry Processional.

Sacred Pause:

A special time which occurs when we are about to make a quantum breakthrough. The door stands open before us. All hindrances have passed. Our passage through this doorway is assured. We know that once we pass through it, nothing will ever be the same again. So we silently sit in the Sacred Pause. This is the moment when we can look backwards at the vast distance we have traveled, seeing everything with enhanced clarity. We can forgive anyone we have harmed, as well as anyone who has hurt us. We can embrace all of our previous experiences with the vastness of our Love. As we do, everything we have known slips away into the realms of the Past That Never Was & the Future Which Never Shall Be. We are finally free! Now it's time to step through the doorway.

See also: Future Which Never Shall Be, Past That Never Was.

Sacred Spiral Dance:

A dance in which two lines of dancers spiral into the center. The dancers embody the Lovers from Beyond the Stars and focus on their partner in the opposite spiral. In the center of the two incoming spirals, the two become the One and spiral outwards as One Being in the Spaces-in-Between. They finally form the spiral of the One Heart. This is an exquisite dance symbolizing the eternal dance of the One Heart. It unifies the opposites into Oneness. It was the key dance performed at the Activation of Second Gate in Ecuador.

There are numerous levels of refinement inherent in this dance. When it is truly danced in the Spaces-In-Between, everything becomes irradiated with a white iridescence and is seen in triplicate. This Dance is the map of our journey from duality into the

realms of the Greater Love. *Also:* It symbolizes the union at the middle point or Equator, of the two spirals of energy emanating from Earth's North and South Poles.
See also: Greater Love, Lovers from Beyond the Stars, One Heart, Sacred Dance, Second Gate, & Spaces-in-Between.

Sacred Union:
The merger into Oneness.

Second Gate:
The Second Gate of the 11:11 was activated on June 5, 1993. The Master Cylinder for this activation was located inside the volcanic crater of Pululahua on the Equator in Ecuador. Serving as gatekeepers for the Second Gate Activation were Isis & Osiris in their final act of service, thus bringing their story to completion. The main themes for the Second Gate are the merger of all polarities into Oneness, the birth of our New Selves and the introduction of the Greater Love. This harmonic is held by the Lovers from Beyond the Stars. *The keynote is:* And the two shall become One.
See also: Doorway of the 11:11, Eleven Gates, First Gate, Greater Love, Isis & Osiris, Lovers from Beyond the Stars, & Third Gate.

Soul Groups:
Groups of beings who share a deep affinity, an alignment of Essence and who have traveled together during our fragmenting process from our larger Group Soul. Soul Groups have worked together throughout history. However, since the Activation of the 11:11 and our subsequent entry into the Invisible, we are now experiencing a dissolving of the ancient Soul Groups. This can be quite painful and confusing at times, but it is leading us to a much greater freedom and deeper Oneness.

Spaces-In-Between:
This refers to leaving behind the old spiral of duality and stepping into the spiral of the Invisible. The Spaces-in-Between are located between the lines of the spiral of duality and are our first immersion into the Invisible.

See also: Invisible, Sacred Spiral Dance, Spirals of Evolution.

Spirals of Evolution:
Pathways of evolution which take the form of spirals. Each time we complete a cycle we return to the point of origin, yet we are on a higher level of the spiral. It's important to remember that we are all traveling on the spiral together. This means that if the spiral turns for one of us, it turns for all of us. It is a reflection of our inherent Oneness. At this time, because of the 11:11 Activation, we have an overlapping of two very different spirals of evolution, one based on duality, the other anchored in Oneness. This gives us the rare opportunity to graduate from duality and shift spirals of evolution. Each of us who steps off the spiral of duality, causes all others remaining in duality to move upwards on the spiral.
See also: Oneness, Spirituality of Duality, Template of Duality, Template of Oneness.

Spirituality of Duality:
The religious and spiritual paths we took to reach the end of the old road of duality. These must now be set aside to travel further into the Unknown. The Spirituality of Duality can enable us to make quantum leaps and ascensions, but only within the evolutionary spiral of duality.
See also: Spirals of Evolution, Template of Duality.

Star-Borne:
Those who originate from the stars. Earth was originally colonized by volunteers from numerous star systems. Each system sent representatives of their finest. This is who we are. We are all Star-Borne. There are simply those who remember, those who are in the process of remembering, and those who choose not to remember at this time.

Star Language:
Languages which come from the stars. There are myriad dialects as there are myriad star systems. Star Language is understood

with the heart, rather than the mind. It is the language of the Invisible as well as the root source of the ancient Earth languages. *See also: Invisible.*

Star Lineage:
Our genealogical linkage to the stars which reflect our inborn, natural affinities and key harmonics. Star lineages are denoted in our Starry Names.
See also: Angel Names, Starry Names.

Starchildren:
The new generation of children being born with their memories intact. Some Starchildren are now in their early twenties; others are still being born. They come here to aid us in our transition from duality to Oneness and will be the leaders of the future.

Starry Councils:
Councils which exist in the realms beyond time and space. We belong to these councils and visit there often, either at night when we are asleep or with our full consciousness. The councils oversee our evolutionary cycles on Earth and within our present Great Central Sun System.

Starry Family:
Those of us who have awakened and are now reuniting in the One Heart throughout the world. The Maori of New Zealand speak of the return of the Star Tribe. This Star Tribe comes from all races of mankind, all countries of the world. They are returning to conscious Oneness. The Star Tribe is our Starry Family.
See also: One Heart, Oneness.

Starry Names:
Our names in Star Language which are in deeper alignment with our Core Selves than our earthly names. They also denote our Star Lineages. A new level of Starry Names is now being discovered. These new names are very short, pure sounds which emanate from the Template of Oneness.

See also: Angel Names, Core Selves, Star Language, Star Lineage, Template of Oneness.

Starry Overself:
Our vast starry Self.

Starry Processional:
The first of our Sacred Dances, the Starry Processional was part of the 11:11 Ceremony and has since been performed around the world. This dance anchors the Template of Oneness. Dancers form a star which slowly revolves to specially created music for twenty-two minutes. The Starry Processional creates double helix energy spirals which anchor the energies into the planet while spiraling deeper into the Invisible.
See also: Doorway of the 11:11, Sacred Dances.

Starry Temples:
Places of initiation which exist in the realms beyond time and space.

Surfing:
The ability to flow upon the subtle currents of the Invisible.
See also: Invisible, Waves of the Invisible.

Template:
A master patterning which governs everything within its sphere causing it to resonate at a similar rate and quality of vibration.
See also: Template of Duality, Template of Oneness.

Template of Duality:
The master patterning or template governing the reality system based on duality. The precepts of duality include: time, space, polarities, separation, limitation & karma.
See also: Template, Template of Oneness.

Template of Oneness:
The master patterning or template governing the Greater Reality system anchored in Oneness.
See also: Oneness, Template.

Third Gate:
The Third Gate of the 11:11 will be activated in 1997. The keynote of this Gate is the establishment of the New Relationships and the creation of Islands of Light.
See also: Doorway of the 11:11, Eleven Gates, First Gate, Islands of Light, Second Gate.

Timing Chain:
The timing mechanism of the Greater Reality. It is composed of two overlaid symbols of the One Heart creating a symbol much like an eye with an upright infinity symbol in the center.

Triangulation:
The method of transcending duality. We establish a third point to the two polarities of duality. This third point is Oneness. The three energies triangulate and merge into a greater One, thus turning duality inside out. "Triangulation is the key for completing duality." *Also:* The process used in unifying our physical eyes with our third eye which leads us to activating the All-Seeing Eye.
See also: All-Seeing Eye of AN, AN, EL•AN•RA, the One, Oneness, Template of Duality.

True Love:
A pure ideal of love which was kept alive, though seldom experienced, throughout our passage in duality. The Template of True Love was finally anchored on Earth at the Temple of Isis on the island of Philae in Egypt on January 17, 1992. This gives us the opportunity to experience the energies of True Love as we travel through the First & Second Gates of the 11:11. Once we enter the Third Gate, we move beyond the realms of True Love into the Greater Love.

*See also: Doorway of the 11:11, First Gate, Greater Love, Isis &
Osiris, Lotus of True Love, Second Gate.*

Unconditional Love:

The highest form of Love found within the Template of Duality. *I
love you.* There is still a separation between *I* and *you.* In the
Template of Oneness, Love simply is. There is never more than
One.
See also: All-Encompassing Love.

Unknown:

That which is unknowable. Once we journey into the Invisible
through the Doorway of the 11:11, we enter the realm of the
Unknown. This means that we have left the familiar comforts
and signposts of our old map. Everything is different here. It is
new and unformed. Our old tools, titles, skills and concepts often have no effect. The Unknown and the Invisible are two aspects of the same place. They both lead to the Greater Reality.
See also: Doorway of the 11:11, Invisible.

Unseen:

What could not be seen or perceived within the Template of
Duality.
See also: the Invisible.

Vertical Energy:

Energy that descends to Earth from On High in a direct, vertical
alignment. Vertical Energy is used to free us from duality by connecting us to the One. In the Template of Oneness, energy could
be described as spiraling circular or all-encompassing. *Also:* First-
hand direct experiences, visions or revelations. Vertical Energy
is always clean and pure.
See also: Horizontal Energy.

Vibrantly Alive:

An ecstatic state of full integration within our physical bodies of
Earth & Star, physical and Invisible, which makes us more alive

than ever before.
See also: Earth-Star, Invisible.

Waves of the Invisible:
The subtle energy currents within the Invisible.
See also: the Invisible, Surfing.

Wild Things:
The Wild Things are nature spirits who live in wild, remote places untouched by humans. They hold an important balance on this planet and should be respected and left alone. Whenever you encounter a place where Wild Things live, you should step aside and not enter their realm. They usually live next to a Fairy Kingdom and serve as protectors for the fairies.

Zone of Overlap:
The doorway created when two dissimilar energy systems are superimposed on each other. This is often of a limited duration and gives us unprecedented opportunities to make mega quantum leaps in consciousness and evolution.
See also: Antarion Conversion, Doorway of the 11:11, EL•AN•RA.

Other Books by Solara

11:11 – *Inside the Doorway* $15.95
A visionary revelation of the 11:11 Cosmology.

EL*AN*RA – *The Healing of Orion*
A wild love story set in the stars containing
the keys to free you from duality! $14.95

The Star-Borne:
A Remembrance for the Awakened Ones
A vast Handbook of Remembrance! $14.95

The Legend of Altazar
A profoundly moving story of Atlantis, Lemuria &
AN to unify your head and heart. $12.95

Invoking Your Celestial Guardians
How to contact & embody your Golden Solar Angel.
$10.00

Also Available:
Videos, Posters T-shirts & more!.

The Starry Messenger
Our light filled newsletter is the Journal of the Invisible.
Yearly subscription: US $25.00   Foreign $30.00

Star-Borne Unlimited
6426 Hwy 93 South #6511
Whitefish, Montana 59937 USA
Phone: (406) 862-8831 • Fax: (406) 862-8851
Web Page: http://www.nvisible.com • email: nvisible@cyberport.net

US Funds only on a US Check or money order.
Please include $3.50 shipping for first item .
50¢ for each additional item. Foreign shipments extra.

Audio Cassettes by Solara
with music by Etherium

The Starry Council $10.00 each
Temple Invisible
True Love/One Heart
Unifying the Polarities
Voyage on the Celestial Barge
Archangel Mikael Empowerment
Star Alignments
Remembering Your Story
The Star That We Are
The Angel You Truly Are

Musical Journeys

The Lotus of True Love
Through the Doorway

Sacred Dance Series *by Etherium & Omashar*

The Earth-Star Dance
The Sacred Spiral Dance
The Greater Central Sun Dance
The Starry Processional

Starry Songs Live!

The Tahitian Star-Borne Reunion
Second Gate in Ecuador
The Australian Star-Borne Reunion